westermann

On Track
Schulaufgabentrainer

Englisch für Gymnasien
Ausgabe Bayern

3

von:
Dunja Reich
Dr. Susanne Auflitsch
Dr. Ulrich Miethaner

herausgegeben von:
Helga Holtkamp

Lehrwerk und weitere Begleitmaterialien:

Schülerbuch ISBN 978-3-14-040803-5
Workbook ISBN 978-3-14-040823-3
Medienpaket ISBN 978-3-14-062675-0
Ferienlektüre ISBN 978-3-14-040883-7

BiBox – Digitale Unterrichtsmaterialien
Nähere Informationen unter www.bibox.schule

Vokabel-Apps sind online erhältlich.

westermann GRUPPE

© 2019 Bildungshaus Schulbuchverlage
Westermann Schroedel Diesterweg Schöningh Winklers GmbH, Braunschweig
www.westermann.de

Das Werk und seine Teile sind urheberrechtlich geschützt.
Jede Nutzung in anderen als den gesetzlich zugelassenen Fällen bedarf der
vorherigen schriftlichen Einwilligung des Verlages.

Auf verschiedenen Seiten dieses Buches finden sich sogenannte Webcodes (Mediencodes).
Die Mediencodes enthalten zusätzliche Unterrichtsmaterialien,
die der Verlag in eigener Verantwortung zur Verfügung stellt.

Druck A[1] / Jahr 2019
Alle Drucke der Serie A sind inhaltlich unverändert.

Redaktion: Dr. Martin Walter
Umschlaggestaltung: Detlef Möller, Paderborn
Umschlagbild vorne: A view of the Skywalk over the Grand Canyon, Arizona, USA; National Geographic Image Collection / Alamy Stock Foto
Umschlagbild hinten: Little Venice with tourist boat, London, England, UK; Kerry Dunstone / Alamy Stock Foto
Druck und Bindung: Westermann Druck GmbH, Braunschweig

ISBN 978-3-14-**040893**-6

Aufbau des Schulaufgabentrainers

Wie ist dein On Track-Schulaufgabentrainer aufgebaut und wie kannst du am besten damit arbeiten?

Dein Schulaufgabentrainer enthält zu jedem der vier Workshops in deinem Buch verschiedene Musterschulaufgaben, mit denen du die gebräuchlichsten Aufgabenformate gezielt üben kannst. Bitte beachte, dass du die Schulaufgaben erst bearbeiten kannst, wenn du den Stoff des gesamten Workshops im Unterricht schon behandelt hast.

Grundsätzlich umfasst jede der hier abgedruckten Schulaufgaben drei Teile aus verschiedenen Bereichen

- *Listening comprehension* (Hörverstehen) oder *Reading comprehension* (Leseverstehen)
- *Use of English,* in mehreren Varianten
- *Mediation* (Sprachmittlung) oder *Writing* (Textproduktion)

Lies dir die folgenden Erklärungen zu den einzelnen Aufgaben gut durch, bevor du anfängst zu üben. Die Tipps werden dir helfen, die Aufgaben sinnvoll zu lösen und so das Üben nachhaltig zu gestalten!

Listening comprehension (Hörverstehen)

Jede Hörverstehensaufgabe, zu der du dir eine Audioaufnahme anhören kannst, ist mit einem Lautsprechersymbol versehen:

Diese Aufnahmen kannst du über einen Webcode abrufen, den du bei jedem Hörtext oben links über dem Lautsprechersymbol findest, z. B. @ SNG-40893-001

Er funktioniert wie eine kleine Webseite. Geh dazu auf die Seite www.westermann.de/webcode und gib den Webcode ohne „@" ein. Als Textformat sind beim Hörverstehen Dialoge üblich, die bezüglich Inhalt, Wortschatz und Strukturen an die im jeweiligen Workshop behandelten Themen angelehnt sind. Es ist nicht ungewöhnlich, dass auch einige unbekannte Wörter vorkommen. Die einzelnen Sprecher und Sprecherinnen sind Muttersprachler, daher haben sie manchmal unterschiedliche Dialekte. Sie sprechen unterschiedlich schnell und verwenden auch umgangssprachliche Ausdrücke und Ausrufe, genauso wie in echten, alltäglichen Gesprächssituationen. Diese Aufgabenformen, die du in deinem Schulaufgabentrainer üben kannst, sind gebräuchlich: Wörter in vorgegebenen Sätzen ergänzen, Informationen ergänzen, Aufgaben zum Ankreuzen (*multiple-choice*), *right-wrong*-Aufgaben zum Ankreuzen, und Fragen zum Text mit freier Antwortmöglichkeit.

> **Folgende Tipps helfen dir, die *listening comprehension*-Aufgaben zu lösen:**
> - Lies vor dem Anhören zuerst alle Fragen durch.
> - Während des ersten Anhörens solltest du einen Bleistift verwenden, um deine Antworten zu skizzieren.
> - In Schulaufgaben ist es üblich, dass du den Hörtext ein zweites Mal anhören darfst. Danach solltest du dich für die endgültigen Antworten entscheiden, indem du mit einem nicht-radierbaren Stift schreibst.

Reading comprehension (Leseverstehen)

Auch beim Leseverstehen (*reading comprehension*) musst du Informationen aus einem dir unbekannten Text entnehmen. Neben beschreibenden Texten oder E-Mails können auch Karten oder Bilder Teil der Aufgabe sein. Da du im Gegensatz zur *listening comprehension* den Text vorliegen hast, ist der Schwierigkeitsgrad höher: Die Texte sind in der Regel länger, es kommen mehr unbekannte Wörter vor und es gibt zusätzliche Aufgabenformen, wie z. B. Fragen, die sich auf das Verständnis des ganzen Textes oder einzelner (unbekannter) Wörter beziehen.

> **Folgende Tipps helfen dir, die *reading comprehension*-Aufgaben zu lösen:**
> - Studiere zunächst alle Fragen genau, denn dann kannst du beim Lesen des Textes gezielt nach den gesuchten Informationen suchen und die entsprechenden Textstellen mit einem (oder mehreren) Textmarker(n) hervorheben.
> - Bei Fragen mit freien Antwortmöglichkeiten musst du Folgendes beachten:
>   - Schreibe ganze Sätze.
>   - Eine Antwort auf eine Frage mit *Why… ?* beginnt nicht mit *Because…!* (Du brauchst davor einen Hauptsatz.)
>   - Vergiss nicht die Unterschiede zwischen einem Fragesatz und einem Aussagesatz im Hinblick auf die Bildung der Zeiten und die Wortstellung. (z. B. When **did** Liam **go** to the cinema? – He **went** …)

Use of English

Der Bereich *use of English* umfasst die Bereiche **Wortschatz**, **Grammatik** und **Sprechabsichten**. In verschiedenen Aufgaben sollst du zeigen, dass du die neu gelernten englischen Ausdrücke und Strukturen, aber auch dein Grundwissen richtig anwenden kannst. In diesen Teilaufgaben erwarten dich neben Lückentexten auch Texte, in denen du Fehler finden und verbessern musst oder Aufgaben mit mehreren Antwortmöglichkeiten (*multiple choice*). Manchmal enthalten die Übungen eine vorgegebene Auswahl der einzusetzenden Verben sowie Hinweise in Klammern. Manche Lücken musst du aber auch ganz ohne Tipps lösen. Bei manchen *use of English*-Aufgaben kannst du zwischen zwei Schwierigkeitsgraden wählen: Bei der *On Track*-Version hast du einige zusätzliche Angaben zur Verfügung, die *Fast Track*-Version ist etwas anspruchsvoller. Du erkennst sie an diesen Symbolen:

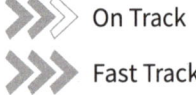 On Track

 Fast Track

> **Folgende Tipps helfen dir, die *use of English*-Aufgaben zu lösen:**
> - Lies dir den Arbeitsauftrag gründlich durch und am besten auch den Lückentext einmal komplett, bevor du beginnst, die Lücken zu füllen.
> - Achte auf die verschiedenen Unterstreichungen der Lücken und deren Erklärung im Arbeitsauftrag.
> - Achte auf den Kontext der Übung und den Rest des lückenhaften Satzes. So erhältst du manchmal wichtige Tipps für die einzusetzende Lösung oder findest auch Signalwörter für die korrekte Zeit.
> - Lies dir die Übung zum Schluss nochmals komplett durch und kontrolliere die von dir eingesetzten Ausdrücke auf Rechtschreibung und Grammatik.

Mediation (Sprachmittlung)

Bei dieser Aufgabenform überträgst du Informationen vom Deutschen sinngemäß, also nicht Wort für Wort, ins Englische. Es gibt im Wesentlichen zwei Formen: Bei der textbasierten *mediation* liegt dir ein englischsprachiger Text vor, z. B. eine E-Mail, ein Interview oder ein Text aus einer Broschüre, aus dem du Informationen entnehmen sollst, an denen eine oder mehrere Personen interessiert sind, die Englisch, aber kein Deutsch können. Bei einer sogenannten Dolmetsch-Übung „vermittelst" du in einem Gespräch zwischen einem Englisch-Sprecher und einem Deutsch-Sprecher. Ein ausführliches Bewertungsraster für *mediation*-Aufgaben findest du hier:

http://www.isb.bayern.de/download/20830/a1_schreiben_lp_.pdf. *Mediation*-Aufgaben sind mit folgendem Symbol gekennzeichnet: M

> **Folgende Tipps helfen dir, die *mediation*-Aufgaben zu lösen:**
> - Lies dir die Aufgabenstellung genau durch: In welcher Situation findet das Gespräch/der Informationsaustausch statt? Wer will was von wem? Was wissen die Beteiligten schon?
> - Übertrage nur die Informationen ins Englische, nach denen auch wirklich gefragt wird.
> - Lass unbekannte Wörter nicht einfach weg! Suche im Deutschen nach einem Wort mit gleicher oder ähnlicher Bedeutung – vielleicht fällt dir ja dazu ein passendes englisches Wort ein. Oft kannst du das unbekannte Wort auch umschreiben.
> - Vergiss nicht, dass du nicht nur die Wörter ins Englische übertragen sollst, sondern dass du auch die Grammatik beachten musst (z. B. richtige Bildung und Verwendung der Zeiten, Satzstellung, usw.). In der Regel erstellen deine Lehrer und Lehrerinnen die Aufgabe so, dass sie auch prüfen, ob du die Grammatik, die du im aktuellen Workshop gelernt hast, in einem zusammenhängenden Text anwenden kannst.

Writing (Textproduktion)

In einem Teil der Schulaufgaben musst du selbst längere, zusammenhängende Texte verfassen. Manchmal musst du dabei z. B. auf eine bereits vorgegebene E-Mail und die darin enthaltenen Fragen antworten. Bitte beachte, dass bei den Textproduktionsaufgaben Inhalt und Sprache getrennt voneinander bewertet werden. Ein ausführliches Bewertungsraster für Aufgaben zur Textproduktion findest du hier: http://www.isb.bayern.de/download/20830/a1_schreiben_lp_.pdf.

> **Folgende Tipps helfen dir, die *writing*-Aufgaben zu lösen:**
> - Lies dir den Arbeitsauftrag gründlich durch und achte darauf, dass dein Text die Vorgaben zur Form, zum Inhalt, zum Adressaten und zur Länge erfüllt.
> - Überlege dir zunächst eine sinnvolle Struktur für deinen Text und mach dir Notizen, z. B. mit einer Mindmap.
> - Verfasse den Text auf Englisch und schreibe eine zur Textsorte passende kurze Einleitung und einen Schluss. Denk bei einer E-Mail an die Anrede und eine freundliche Verabschiedung.
> - Versuche deine Sätze flüssig miteinander zu verbinden, indem du *linking words* wie *and*, *because*, *or* usw. beziehungsweise Strukturwörter wie *First,… Then…* oder *Finally,…* verwendest.
> - Versuche Wiederholungen und häufige Wörter wie *thing* oder *make* zu vermeiden und verwende viele Adjektive, um deinen Text anschaulich und lebhaft zu gestalten.
> - Achte auf vollständige Sätze und besonders auf die korrekte englische Satzstellung (S-V-O!).
> - Lies deinen fertigen Text zweimal durch. Achte beim ersten Durchgang nur auf den Inhalt und den Sinn des Textes. Beim zweiten Durchgang kontrollierst du den Text auf die sprachliche Richtigkeit.

Schulaufgabenvorbereitung: Allgemeine Tipps

- Nimm dir an jedem Lerntag einen Teil der neuen Grammatik schwerpunktmäßig vor. Lies dir den Eintrag im Grammatikteil des Lehrbuchs (S. 150ff.) nochmals aufmerksam durch und wiederhole die gemachten Übungen.
- Lerne die Vokabeln kontinuierlich und gewissenhaft mit. Dreimal fünf Minuten über den Tag verteilt zu üben, ist dabei effektiver als einmal fünfzehn Minuten! Dazu kannst du auch die *Wordary*-Seiten im Workbook oder die Vokabel-App von Phase6 nutzen (https://www.phase-6.de/classic/lerninhalte/Schoningh/Englisch/On-Track-Bayern/).

Vorwort

- Wiederhole die Vokabeln vor der Schulaufgabe über mindestens 10 Tage verteilt in kleineren Portionen.
- Notiere diejenigen Wörter, die du dir schwer merken kannst, auf neuen Karteikarten oder einem speziellen Übungsblatt und übe sie täglich.
- Denk daran, die neuen Wörter unbedingt auch handschriftlich zu üben, damit dein Gehirn das richtige Schriftbild abspeichern kann.
- Wiederhole die Lektionstexte mithilfe der im Schülerbuch abgedruckten Webcodes und der Lesetexte.

Das On Track-Team wünscht dir viel Erfolg bei der Vorbereitung!

Inhalt

Seite	Inhalte
3–6	Vorwort: Konzeption und Aufbau
Schulaufgabe 1 (Workshop 1, 80 CP)	
9	Listening comprehension: A radio podcast (20 CP)
10	Use of English: A school council report (*On Track*, 30 CP)
12	Use of English: A school council report (*Fast Track*, 30 CP)
13	Mediation: Einladung zur SMV-Versammlung (30 CP)
Schulaufgabe 2 (Workshop 1, 80 CP)	
16	Writing: An email to the head teacher (30 CP)
17	Use of English: At the museum (*On Track*, 30 CP)
18	Use of English: At the museum (*Fast Track*, 30 CP)
21	Reading comprehension: Upcycling (20 CP)
Schulaufgabe 3 (Workshop 2, 85 CP)	
24	Reading comprehension: A newspaper article (25 CP)
27	Use of English: A new world (*On Track*, 30 CP)
28	Use of English: A new world (*Fast Track*, 30 CP)
29	Writing: Thanksgiving (30 CP)
Schulaufgabe 4 (Workshop 2, 80 CP)	
30	Listening comprehension: Family history (20 CP)
32	Use of English: A footballer from Hill End School (*On Track*, 30 CP)
33	Use of English: A footballer from Hill End School (*Fast Track*, 30 CP)
34	Mediation: Die Bretter, die die Welt bedeuten (30 CP)
Schulaufgabe 5 (Workshop 3, 80 CP)	
38	Reading comprehension: The Afanc (20 CP)
41	Use of English: A trip to Llangollen (*On Track*, 30 CP)
42	Use of English: A trip to Llangollen (*Fast Track*, 30 CP)
44	Writing: A holiday in Wales (30 CP)
Schulaufgabe 6 (Workshop 3, 86 CP)	
45	Listening comprehension: The Red Lion (20 CP)
46	Use of English: Famous Welshmen and Welshwomen (*On Track*, 36 CP)
49	Use of English: Famous Welshmen and Welshwomen (*Fast Track*, 36 CP)
52	Mediation: Osterferien in Bayern (30 CP)
Schulaufgabe 7 (Workshop 4, 84 CP)	
54	Listening comprehension: Welcome to Denver, Colorado! (24 CP)
55	Use of English: The Grand Canyon (*On Track*, 30 CP)
57	Use of English: The Grand Canyon (*Fast Track*, 30 CP)
59	Mediation: Die Umwelt-AG (30 CP)

Seite	Inhalte
Schulaufgabe 8 (Workshop 4, 88 CP)	
61	Reading comprehension: Lilac's blog (24 CP)
66	Use of English: My favorite holiday (*On Track*, 34 CP)
68	Use of English: My favorite holiday (*Fast Track*, 34 CP)
70	Writing: A gap year in the American Southwest (30 CP)
Zusatzmaterial	
71	Audioskripte
75	Answer key

Schulaufgabe 1

Workshop 1
→ students' book, pp. 14 – 20

Schulaufgabe 1 (80 CP)

1 Listening comprehension: A radio podcast (20 CP)

You are going to listen to a podcast of Hill End School FM, the school's radio station.

1 Who? What? Tick the correct combination. (8 CP)

	Henry	Aimee	Polly	Simon	Lily	Lucas	none of them
1 … likes the new project.	☐	☐	☐	☐	☐	☐	☐
2 … is not going to take part in the new project.	☐	☐	☐	☐	☐	☐	☐
3 … presents the podcast.	☐	☐	☐	☐	☐	☐	☐
4 … has interviewed students at Hill End School.	☐	☐	☐	☐	☐	☐	☐
5 … wants to collect money for the project.	☐	☐	☐	☐	☐	☐	☐
6 … is the most important member of the school council.	☐	☐	☐	☐	☐	☐	☐

2 Choose the correct diagram. Which of the following diagrams shows the result of the school council's survey? Tick the correct option and add the missing numbers to the correct diagram. (3 CP)

Survey: Would you like to protect our nature and support the school council's project 'Hill End School goes green'? ■ yes ■ no

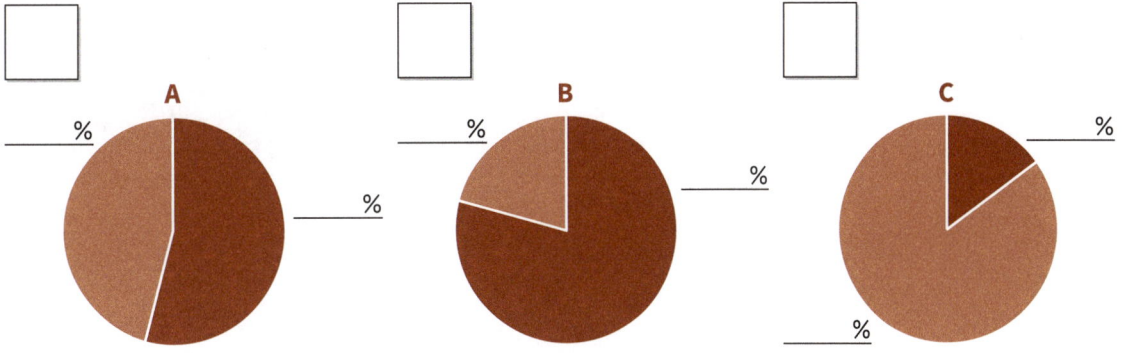

Schulaufgabe 1   Workshop 1
→ students' book, pp. 14–20

3 Add the missing information or number. (2 CP)

Up to now, _____ students want to take part in the project.

Those who want to join 'Hill End School goes green' can sign up on the school council's

_____ .

4 Choose the correct answer(s). Several options can be correct. (7 CP)

Simon ☐ wants to have less books because his schoolbag is too heavy.
       ☐ wants to get less printed worksheets.
       ☐ wants to ban plastic bottles at his school.
       ☐ thinks that digital books help to protect our nature.
       ☐ has signed up via email.
       ☐ thinks that laptops will be less expensive than books if they are used for several years.

Lily   ☐ likes exotic vegetables.
       ☐ is a vegetarian.
       ☐ prefers regional products.
       ☐ thinks that buying vegetables on a farm helps reduce plastic waste.
       ☐ has got a button with the project's slogan.

Lucas ☐ has got a button with the project's slogan.
       ☐ thinks that busses are bad for the environment.
       ☐ usually goes to school by bike.
       ☐ wants the students to walk to school.
       ☐ doesn't like parents who take their children to school by car.

›› 2 Use of English: A school council report (On Track; 30 CP)

Aimee has written a report about the activities of the school council for the latest issue of the school magazine.

_____   → Please fill in the missing word(s) in English.

....   → Please fill in the verbs in the correct form. (x = negative form).

At our last meeting, the members of the school council ....

(*talk*) about their activities, plans and ideas. Life at our school ....

.... (*already / improve*) a lot, but some problems

Schulaufgabe 1 — Workshop 1

→ students' book, pp. 14–20

_____ (yet / solve / x).

Let's start with the _____ (= the process of sth. becoming better): The principal _____ (already / ban) _____ (= bad for your body) food and _____ (≠ glass) bottles from our canteen and the school _____ (buy) more computers for the library.

However, the principal _____ (react / x) to our last wish list yet, which means that the text for the school's website about our charity event _____ (so far / write / x) and that the students who _____ (never / travel) to Germany before still _____ (know / x) if they can take part in this year's exchange programme.

At the moment the school council _____ (plan) to start a new project called 'Helping Hands at Hill End School', _____ could create many chances to take r_____y (→ noun: responsible). Students from our school can help old people, for example they can do the shopping or take their dogs for a walk. Last week we _____ (meet) the principal who _____ (say): 'I'm sure that this project _____ (turn out) to be a big _____ (= when you have achieved a good result) very soon and that the people will be very _____ (= feeling or showing thanks) in the future.'

As you know Durham _____ (choose) a new _____ (= head of a town) in the _____ (= vote) last Sunday and we _____ (already / analyse) the promises he _____ (so far / make) during his _____ (= time as a candidate). We are going to meet him next Thursday, but instead of chatting, we are going to c_____ (= ask tricky questions) him in an interview because we want to learn more about his _____ (= what he thinks) on topics which are important for the younger generation.

Let's see if he's still the c_____ (= feeling sure) person he _____ (so far / be). If there are any questions you would like us to ask him, send us an email (schoolcouncil@hillendschool.co.uk).

Schulaufgabe 1 — Workshop 1

→ students' book, pp. 14–20

⇒⇒⇒ 2 Use of English: A school council report (Fast Track; 30 CP)

Aimee has written another report about the activities of the school council for the latest issue of the school magazine.

_____ → Please fill in the missing word(s) in English.

.... → Please fill one of the following verbs and the signal words in brackets. (x = negative form). You can use the verbs more than once.

> analyse ■ ban ■ buy ■ choose ■ improve ■ know ■
> make ■ meet ■ plan ■ react ■ say ■ solve ■ talk ■ travel ■
> turn ■ write

At our last meeting, the members of the school council .... about their activities, plans and ideas. Life at our school .... (*already*) a lot, but some problems .... (*x / yet*).

Let's start with the _____ (= *the process of sth becoming better*): The principal .... (*already*) _____ (= *bad for your body*) food and _____ (≠ *glass*) bottles from our canteen and the school .... more computers for the library.

However, the principal .... (*x*) to our last wish list yet, which means that the text for the school's website about our charity event .... (*x / so far*) and that the students who .... (*never*) to Germany before still .... (*x*) if they can take part in this year's exchange programme.

At the moment the school council .... to start a new project called 'Helping Hands at Hill End School', _____ could create many chances to take _____ (→ *noun: responsible*).

Students from our school can help old people, for example they can do the shopping or take their dogs for a walk. Last week we .... the principal who ....: 'I'm sure that this project .... out to be a big _____ (= *when you have achieved a good result*) very soon and that the people will be very _____ (= *feeling or showing thanks*) in the future.'

Schulaufgabe 1 — Workshop 1

→ students' book, pp. 14–20

As you know Durham .... a new .... (= *head of a town*) in the .... (= *vote*) last Sunday and we .... (*already*) the promises he .... so far during his .... (= *time as a candidate*). We are going to meet him next Thursday, but instead of chatting, we are going to .... (= *ask tricky questions*) him in an interview because we want to learn more about his .... (= *what he thinks*) on topics which are important for the younger generation. Let's see if he's still the .... (= *feeling sure*) person he .... (*so far*). If there are any questions you would like us to ask him, send us an email (schoolcouncil@hillendschool.co.uk).

M 3 Mediation: Einladung zur SMV-Versammlung (30 CP)

Deine englische Austauschpartnerin Sophie ist vor kurzem in Deutschland angekommen und besucht heute zum ersten Mal deine Schule. Während des Rundgangs durch eure Schule kommt ihr an dem folgenden Plakat der SMV vorbei. Leider versteht sie die Informationen nur teilweise und bittet dich deshalb um Hilfe. Beantworte ihre Fragen auf Englisch in ganzen Sätzen. Verwende dazu die Informationen des Plakats und deinen Stundenplan.

Die
SMV
lädt alle Mitglieder und diejenigen Schülerinnen und Schüler, die es werden wollen, ein zur

1. SMV-Versammlung
dieses Schuljahres.

Datum: Dienstag, 5. Oktober
Uhrzeit: Mittagspause und 8. Stunde (13.10 – 14.40 Uhr)
Ort: Turnhalle

Tagesordnung:
1) Wahl der neuen Schülersprecher
2) Planung des Weihnachtskonzerts der SMV
3) Prämierung des besten Schullogos und Vorstellung der neuen SMV-Kollektion (Kapuzenpullis, Federmäppchen und Taschen), die mit diesem Logo bedruckt ist.

Weitere Themen, die im Rahmen dieser Versammlung besprochen werden sollen, können gerne vorab per E-Mail eingereicht werden, am besten mit einer kurzen Erläuterung des konkreten Anliegens. Bitte sendet eure Vorschläge an smv@abc-gymnasium.de.

Eine Unterrichtsbefreiung für die Teilnahme an der Versammlung kann nur nach Rücksprache mit der betreffenden Lehrkraft und der Schulleitung erfolgen.

Schulaufgabe 1

Workshop 1
→ students' book, pp. 14–20

Uhrzeit	Montag	Dienstag	Mittwoch	Donnerstag	Freitag
08.00–08.45	Mathematik	Deutsch	Englisch	Deutsch	Französisch
08.45–09.30	Französisch	Englisch	Englisch	Religion/Ethik	Französisch
	PAUSE				
09.45–10.30	Englisch	Geographie	Musik	Mathematik	Deutsch
10.30–11.15	Kunst	Französisch	Deutsch	Englisch	Deutsch
	PAUSE				
11.30–12.15	Deutsch	Mathematik	Kunst	Sport	Musik
12.15–13.00	Religion/Ethik	Sport	Mathematik	Sport	Mathematik
13.10–13.55	MITTAGSPAUSE				
13.55–14.40		Geschichte		Tischtennis	Schach
14.45–15.30		Informatik			

Sophie   I really like your school, but the building is huge! And there are posters everywhere … I guess that there are lots of great events, but I don't understand most of the information. What about this poster, what is it about?

You   _____
_____
_____
_____

Sophie   When and where does this meeting take place?

You   _____
_____
_____
_____

Sophie   What are the members of the school council going to do or talk about?

You   _____
_____
_____
_____

Sophie   Sounds interesting. Can we go there, too?

You   1 _____ because _____
_____

       2 _____ because _____
_____

© Westermann Gruppe

Schulaufgabe 1

Workshop 1
→ students' book, pp. 14–20

Sophie   Oh, what a pity! I'm sure that many students who can't go there have good ideas, too. But their ideas won't be heard…

You   Students who have a good idea or suggestion can _____

_____

_____

_____

Sophie   Alright, so let's continue our tour of the school building. Maybe we'll find some good ideas …

© Westermann Gruppe

Schulaufgabe 2 (80 CP)

1 Writing: An email to the head teacher (30 CP)

You are taking part in an exchange programme with Jonathan and it's your last day at your exchange partner's school. You've just had lunch in the canteen with Jonathan's classmates but you are quite unhappy. You think of your canteen at home, which is quite different, so you ask your exchange partner to help you write an email to his head teacher in which you tell him about your ideas and why the changes are necessary. Write a letter of about 120 – 150 words on an extra sheet.

These are the things you want to change:

Schulaufgabe 2 — Workshop 1

→ students' book, pp. 12–21

  Use of English: At the museum (On Track; 30 CP)

Aimee and Mrs Gordon are waiting for Mr Gordon at the entrance of the museum. Aimee is quite angry. Make sentences and put the verbs in the correct form.

Aimee   Why doesn't dad look at his mobile phone and read his messages?

him | four text messages | already | I | to send | !

_____

Mrs Gordon   Oh look, there he is… Finally!

Aimee   to be | where | you | Dad | ?

_____

Mr Gordon   to visit | the museum | just | I | .

_____

What a wonderful exhibition!

yet | to see | the great paintings | you | ?

_____

Aimee   Yes, I have.

Mrs Gordon   the tour | this morning | you | where | to start | ?

_____

Mr Gordon   second floor | I | first | to go to | .

_____

lunch | to have | I | at the cafeteria | then | .

_____

Mrs Gordon   Without us? Why?

Mr Gordon   Sorry, dear. You seem to be quite upset.

you | to wait for | how long | me | ?

_____

Aimee   to sit | we | here | since 1 o'clock | !

_____

my text messages | not | why | you | to read | ?

_____

© Westermann Gruppe

Schulaufgabe 2 — Workshop 1

→ students' book, pp. 12–21

Mr Gordon   I'm sorry but

in the car | my mobile phone | to forget | I | .

_____

_____

to do | you | what | until now | ?

_____

_____

Aimee   for half an hour | the audio guide | I | to listen to | .

_____

_____

Mum | since half past one | her book | to read | .

_____

_____

Mr Gordon   Which book?

Aimee   The book which

in the shop | to buy | she | when | to leave | without you | we | the museum | .

_____

_____

Mr Gordon   I'm really sorry. Do you want to come back to the second floor with me?

The paintings there are fascinating!

Aimee   Oh no, Dad! I want to go home!

 2 Use of English: At the museum (Fast Track; 30 CP)

Aimee and Mrs Gordon are waiting for Mr Gordon at the entrance of the museum. Aimee is quite angry. Make sentences and put the verbs in the correct form.

☆ = *since* or *for*?

◆ = add the missing word

Aimee   Why doesn't dad look at his mobile phone and read his messages?

him | four text messages | already | I | to send | !

_____

_____

Schulaufgabe 2 — Workshop 1

→ students' book, pp. 12–21

Mrs Gordon Oh look, there he is... Finally!

Aimee to be | where | you | Dad | ?

_____

_____

Mr Gordon to visit | the museum | just | I | .

_____

_____

What a wonderful exhibition!

yet | to see | the great paintings | you | ?

_____

_____

Aimee Yes, I have.

Mrs Gordon the tour | this morning | you | where | to start | ?

_____

_____

Mr Gordon second floor | I | first | to go ◆ | .

_____

_____

lunch | to have | I | at the cafeteria | then | .

_____

_____

Mrs Gordon Without us? Why?

Mr Gordon Sorry, dear. You seem to be quite upset?

you | to wait ◆ | how long | me | ?

_____

_____

Aimee to sit | we | here | ☆ 1 o'clock | !

_____

_____

my text messages | not | why | so far | you | to read | ?

_____

_____

Schulaufgabe 2 — Workshop 1
→ students' book, pp. 12–21

Mr Gordon I'm sorry but

◆ the car | my mobile phone | to forget | I | .
_____
_____

to do | you | what | until now | ?
_____
_____

Aimee ☆ half an hour | the audio guide | I | to listen ◆ | .
_____
_____

Mum | ☆ half past one | her book | to read | .
_____
_____

Mr Gordon Which book?

Aimee The book which

in the shop | to buy | she | when | to leave | without you | we | the museum | .
_____
_____

Mr Gordon I'm really sorry. Do you want to come back to the second floor with me?

The paintings there are fascinating!

Aimee Oh no, Dad! I want to go home!

Schulaufgabe 2

Workshop 1
→ students' book, pp. 22/23

3 Reading comprehension: Upcycling (20 CP)

The school council at Hill End School has organized an interesting project. Deepak writes about it in a forum and asks for advice. Read the texts and answer the following questions.

Deepak — 12 October 18:27

Hi everyone,
I've recently become a member of our school council because I like to work with young people who want to improve things, not only at school but in general. Lots of students at my school want to fight against pollution and we all have a dream that we can make our town greener.

That's the reason why we organized a fantastic event last Saturday. Many of our students, their families and our teachers helped us collect waste in Durham. It was really scary because we realized that people had left the things they didn't need anymore almost everywhere: next to the roads, under the bushes in the park, in the city centre and even in the river!

The result is both surprising and sad: 63 huge bags which are full of plastic bottles, old newspapers, cardboard boxes, carton[1] packaging, and so on. The craziest things we've found are a broken bike, a hat, old shoes and a mobile phone which doesn't work anymore. Actually, we don't just want to recycle all the rubbish, we would like to be more creative. Can anyone think of a great idea? I'd be really grateful …

Caroline — 12 October 18:53

Of course there are more creative ways than recycling. Have you ever heard of 'upcycling'? It means that you turn useless or broken things into something new, something more creative and useful or nice. For example, you could use the plastic bottles as containers for small things like buttons or pins. Just cut off the top of the bottle, colour it in a fancy way and fill it with whatever you like!

Jeremy — 12 October 19:11

I absolutely disagree with you. Why should this rubbish still be around? You should sort the waste and recycle it as quickly as possible. Make people aware of the fact that they should avoid all the plastic packaging in the first place!

Sharon — 12 October 19:23

I like upcycling, too, and I usually turn plastic and metal objects into jewellery. My favourite necklace used to be a coffee capsule[2] and my earrings include parts of old toys. I've already sold these upcycled objects and given the money to charity organizations.

Martin — 12 October 19:41

I totally understand what you mean, Deepak. Why don't you use the craziest objects which you've found for a statue or huge object?

---

[1] **carton** a box or container, for example used for drinks
[2] **capsule** Kapsel

Schulaufgabe 2 — Workshop 1

→ students' book, pp. 22/23

Deepak 12 October 19:59

Wow, that's an amazing idea! If we put the statue in front of our school building, we are reminded of the waste problem every day, and, Jeremy, maybe it makes people think about the products they buy, use and throw away …

1 Which of the following projects are possible? Deepak can only use the things which he has mentioned in the text! Choose two correct pictures and explain why the other pictures are wrong. (4 CP)

☐ Yes, he can make this statue.

☐ No, he can't make this statue because
_____

☐ Yes, he can make this because

☐ No, he can't make this because
_____

☐ Yes, he can make this car.

☐ No, he can't make this car because
_____

☐ Yes, he can make this chair and table

☐ No, he can't make this chair and table because
_____

Schulaufgabe 2

Workshop 1

→ students' book, pp. 22/23

2 **Who thinks that … ?** Tick (✓) six correct combinations. You can choose more than one person for the sentences. (6 CP)

Who thinks that …	Deepak	Caroline	Jeremy	Sharon	Martin	Not in the text
… there should be less pollution in his or her home town.	☐	☐	☐	☐	☐	☐
… it's a good idea to use old things again in a different way.	☐	☐	☐	☐	☐	☐
… people who leave plastic bags in a park should be reported to the police.	☐	☐	☐	☐	☐	☐

3 **Tick (✓) the right answers.** (5 CP)

1 Tick two correct answers: Deepak wants to …

☐ turn Hill End School into a greener school.
☐ reduce the number of plastic bottles at his school.
☐ protect our nature.
☐ actively change situations which he doesn't like.

2 Tick three correct answers: He and his friends found waste which …

☐ has been thrown out of a car.
☐ you could eat.
☐ was wet.
☐ was very dangerous.
☐ was very heavy.
☐ was difficult to see.

4 **Right or wrong or not in the text?** (5 CP)

	right	wrong	not in the text
1 'Upcycling' means that you simply repair something.	☐	☐	☐
2 Caroline has never used old clothes for upcycling.	☐	☐	☐
3 Caroline wants to use plastic bottles in her garden.	☐	☐	☐
4 Jeremy wants people to buy products which don't need a lot of plastic.	☐	☐	☐
5 Sharon likes to help poor people with her creative ideas.	☐	☐	☐

© Westermann Gruppe

Schulaufgabe 3 (85 CP)

1 Reading comprehension: A newspaper article (25 CP)

More and more people would like to celebrate Thanksgiving in Germany, too, so you want to find out more about this American tradition. You have found the following article in a newspaper. Read the text carefully and answer the questions.

A _____

B _____

The first real American Thanksgiving ceremony was held by the Pilgrim Fathers of Massachusetts at Plymouth Rock in 1621. A Native American named Squanto brought the starving settlers a present of wild turkey, fruit, fish and vegetables. He also taught them how to hunt and how to grow crops. The pilgrims thanked the Lord for their deliverance[1], and gave a big party for the Native Americans, which they called *Thanksgiving*.
This celebration became a symbol of friendship between white people and Native Americans, and the turkey became a symbol of plenty[2]. In 1861, Abraham Lincoln made Thanksgiving a national holiday, but he did not fix a date. In 1941, however, President Theodore Roosevelt decided that Thanksgiving should be held on the last Thursday in November. Most people also take the Friday off, so that they can spend a long weekend with family and friends.

C _____

The Americans love to eat well, and a traditional Thanksgiving dinner is a real treat[3]. The main dish is usually a stuffed turkey served with lots of vegetables and fruit. Cranberry sauce and corn on the cob are standard, but sweet potatoes and red cabbage are also very popular. Vegetarians can have 'tofurkey' made of tofu; but meat eaters with big appetites can also buy a 'turducken', a turkey stuffed[4] with a duck stuffed with a small chicken. After a heavy dinner, you can look forward to the most American of all desserts: a juicy pumpkin pie.

D _____

Thanksgiving would not be complete without American football. Most American families watch the NFL Thanksgiving Classic on TV. American football is almost a religion, and at Thanksgiving it often replaces churchgoing and prayer.

E _____

Some turkeys are luckier than others. Americans eat around 41 million of the big birds on Thanksgiving Day alone. In 1947, however, the Poultry and Egg National Board gave President Harry Truman a present of three turkeys. Two were killed for a White House dinner, but one was given a presidential pardon and was sent to a lovely little farm to spend the rest of his life in peace. The turkey pardon is an important symbolic act to remind people that the American President is both powerful and merciful[5].

---

[1] **deliverance** *Erlösung*
[2] **plenty** wealthy, rich
[3] **treat** a delicious meal
[4] **stuffed** filled
[5] **merciful** if you can forgive somebody

F _____

Thanksgiving officially celebrates the friendship between the Native Americans and white people. However, as we know, America's colonisation by white settlers was horrible for the native population. Millions of people died of European diseases and many were murdered by white settlers. Even today, America's natives are the poorest ethnic group in the US. On Thanksgiving Day, a group of Native Americans gather at Plymouth Rock to mourn and fast in honour of all the Native Americans who died because of colonialism.

1 **Find a good heading for the article (A) and the different paragraphs (B – F).** Choose from the following box. (6 CP)

> Anti-Thanksgiving campaigns ■ Family and Friends ■ Food ■ Football ■ History ■ Plymouth Rock ■ Problems ■ Thanksgiving: an all-American party for the whole family ■ Turkey Pardon

2 **Right or wrong or not in the text?** (7 CP)

		right	wrong	not in the text
1	The tradition of Thanksgiving began in the 16th century.	☐	☐	☐
2	It started with a Native American who helped people from England who were very hungry.	☐	☐	☐
3	He told the new settlers not to kill any animals.	☐	☐	☐
4	He helped them even though he didn't understand their language.	☐	☐	☐
5	The first ceremony was organised by the Native Americans to welcome the new settlers.	☐	☐	☐
6	The tradition of Thanksgiving reminds us of the good relationship between Native Americans and the early English settlers.	☐	☐	☐
7	Thanks to Theodore Roosevelt, most Americans don't have to go to work or to school on Thanksgiving.	☐	☐	☐

3 **When are we going to celebrate Thanksgiving?** Circle the right date in this calendar (1 CP).

November						
M	T	W	T	F	S	S
	1	2	3	4	5	6
7	8	9	10	11	12	13
14	15	16	17	18	19	20
21	22	23	24	25	26	27
28	29	30				

Schulaufgabe 3 — Workshop 2
→ students' book, pp. 56/57

4 Tick (✓) the right answers. Sometimes more than one answer is correct. (5 CP)

1 According to the text there are special dishes …
☐ for Native Americans.
☐ for people who prefer sweet dishes.
☐ for people who want to eat a lot of meat.
☐ for children.
☐ for people who are allergic to meat.
☐ for people who don't want to eat meat.

2 According to the text some people think that …
☐ big sport events are more important on Thanksgiving than going to church.
☐ it's important to thank God and to go to church on Thanksgiving.
☐ people need to do sports after Thanksgiving.
☐ it's fun to play American football with your friends on Thanksgiving.

3 In 1947, Harry Truman …
☐ didn't want to have a turkey.
☐ decided that no turkeys should be killed for Thanksgiving.
☐ received two turkeys as a gift.
☐ received three turkeys as a gift.
☐ decided that one of his turkeys shouldn't be killed.
☐ made Thanksgiving a national holiday.

5 Answer the following questions. Write complete sentences. (6 CP)

1 In your own words, explain the expression 'Turkey Pardon' and what it stands for.
_____
_____
_____
_____

2 Which negative consequences resulted from American colonisation for the Native Americans? Use the information given in the text. (three aspects)
_____
_____
_____
_____
_____
_____

Schulaufgabe 3 — Workshop 2
→ students' book, pp. 44-47

2 Use of English: A new world (On Track; 30 CP)

Complete the text.

- - - - - - - - - → Complete the missing word.

_____ → Add one of the adjectives in the box.
Be careful: adjective or adverb?

Most of the children of our g e n _ _ _ _ _ _ _ _ in the USA know the famous story about their a n _ _ _ _ _ _ _ _ and their _ _ _ g i n, which they can find in almost every history _ _ _ t b _ _ _ _ :

| brave ■ European ■ happy ■ religious |

In the past, many _____ people went on a v o _ _ _ _ _ (= trip) to the New World. Among them there were _ x p _ _ _ _ _ _ _ who wanted to discover the New World, _____ s _ t _ _ _ _ _ _ who wanted to build new c o _ _ _ _ _ _ _ _, s _ _ v a _ _ _ who wanted to have a better life in freedom and _____ people who left England because of their b e _ _ _ _ _ s. All of them wanted to live _____ in p _ _ _ _ (≠ war) and without h _ _ _ _ _ _ (= with enough food).

| certain ■ dangerous ■ long ■ nervous ■ quick ■ rough |

The _____ journey by ship was usually very _____ and _____. At the beginning, all the people on the d _ _ _ of the ship were s t r _ _ _ _ _ _ who had _____ left their families, but they _____ got to know each other very _____.

| anxious ■ good ■ hard ■ slow ■ successful |

When they _____ arrived in the New World, the s _ _ v _ _ _ _ _ of the journey _____ left the ship. During the following years they usually got on quite _____, they worked very _____ and _____ improved their new lives.

Schulaufgabe 3 — Workshop 2
→ students' book, pp. 44-47

››› 2 Use of English: A new world (Fast Track; 30 CP)

Complete the text.

‑ ‑ ‑ ‑ ‑ ‑ ‑ ‑ ‑ ‑ → Please complete the missing word correctly.

_____ → Add one of the adjectives below. There are more adjectives than you need. Be careful: adjective or adverb?

anxious ■ bad ■ brave ■ calm ■ careful ■ certain ■ dangerous ■ easy ■ European ■ fast ■ good ■ happy ■ hard ■ long ■ loud ■ nervous ■ quick ■ religious ■ rough ■ slow ■ successful

Most of the children of our g e n _ _ _ _ _ _ _ _ in the USA know the famous story about their a n _ _ _ _ _ _ _ _ and their _ _ _ g i n , which they can find in almost every history _ _ x t _ _ _ _ :

In the past, many _____ people went on a v o _ _ _ _ to the New World. Among them there were _ _ p _ _ _ _ _ _ _ who wanted to discover the New World, _____ s _ _ _ _ _ _ _ who wanted to start new c _ _ _ _ _ _ _ _ , _ _ _ v _ _ _ _ _ who wanted to have a better life in freedom and _____ people who left England because of their b _ _ _ _ _ s . All of them wanted to live _____ in p _ _ _ _ without any wars and without h _ _ _ _ _ _ .

The _____ journey by ship was usually very _____ and _____ . At the beginning, all the people on the d _ _ _ of the ship were s t _ _ _ _ _ _ _ who _____ left their families, but they _____ got to know each other very _____ .

When they _____ arrived in the New World, the s _ _ v _ _ _ _ _ _ of the journey _____ left the ship. During the following years they usually got on quite _____ , they worked very _____ and _____ improved their new lives.

3 Writing: Thanksgiving (30 CP)

You have found the following entry on a forum on the Internet. As you know a lot about the history of the United States, you can answer the questions in English. Write a text of about 120 words. Use at least 15 of the following expressions in your text.

> calmly ■ differently ■ exciting ■ fishing ■ grow food ■ hunting ■ interpreter ■ Mayflower ■ Native Americans ■ nervously ■ North America ■ to own the land ■ Patuxet ■ plague ■ to plant crops ■ Plymouth ■ Squanto ■ terribly ■ Treaty of Friendship ■ Wampanoag: 'People of the Light'

Hi everybody!

I've just watched a movie in which an American family celebrated Thanksgiving. I've got the impression that it is almost the same as Christmas in Europe … But what does it have to do with Native Americans and the Europeans who came to North America in the 17th century?

Thanks for your reply in advance!

CharlieCucumber08315

Schulaufgabe 4

Workshop 2
→ students' book, pp. 44-47

Schulaufgabe 4 (80 CP)

1 Listening comprehension: Family history (20 CP)

The project on American history has shown Vivian that most of her friends are the descendants of immigrants from all over the world. Today she's talking to her best friend's mum, Sarah O'Brian. Listen to the text twice and answer the following questions.

1 What's the date today and why is it a special day for Shauna's family?
Complete the calendar. (3 CP)

Month:	_____
Day:	_____
	Don't forget: It's _____ _____!

2 Where did Shauna's ancestors come from?
Circle the country or region on the following map. (1 CP)

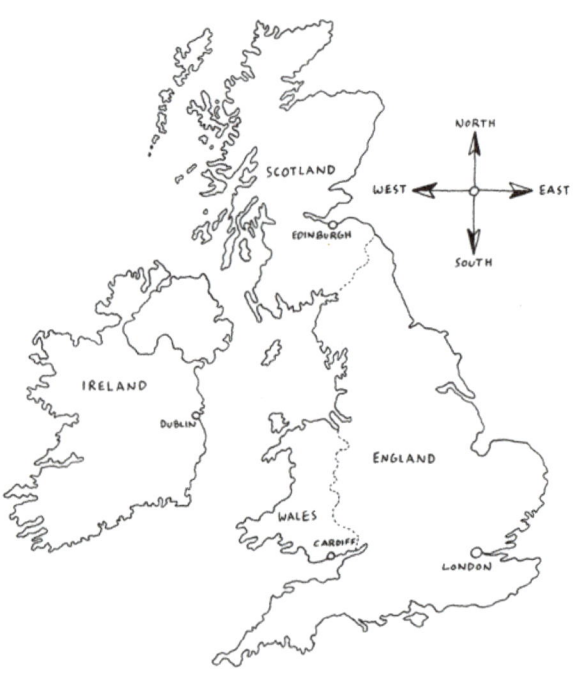

Schulaufgabe 4 — Workshop 2

→ students' book, pp. 44-47

3 A timeline of Conor's life. Fill in the missing dates. (4 CP)

year	event
_____	Conor was born.
_____ - _____	'Great Famine'
_____	Conor emigrated to the USA.

4 Tick (✓) the two correct answers. (2 ✓ = 2 CP)

Conor's life was very difficult before he went to the USA because …
☐ the supermarket was too far away.
☐ there was not enough food.
☐ all the animals on his parents' farm had died.
☐ his family was very poor.
☐ his family had to sell the fields.
☐ he didn't find a job.

5 How did Conor travel to the USA? (2 CP)

☐   ☐   ☐   ☐

6 Right or wrong? (4 CP)

		right	wrong
1	Conor travelled without any of the other members of his family.	☐	☐
2	The journey was very dangerous right from the start.	☐	☐
3	Mrs O'Brian knows a lot about his journey from the letters he sent to his family.	☐	☐
4	The journey took 34 days.	☐	☐

7 Conor's new life in the USA. Fill in the missing words. (4 CP)

Conor started a new life in the USA, where he worked as a _____ .

When he was _____ years old, he started a family with his wife

Andrea, who was of _____ origin. Shauna's family loves some of her

traditions, too, especially the delicious _____ .

Schulaufgabe 4 — Workshop 2
→ students' book, pp. 58/59

2 Use of English: A footballer from Hill End School (On Track)

Mixed Bag (30 CP)

_____ → Please fill in the missing word(s).
~~my book~~ → Please use a possessive pronoun to replace the expression.
☐ → Please choose the correct option.

James is one of the best football players at Hill End School.
He started to play ☐ more early than
☐ earlier than
☐ the earliest as

his friends. He can kick the ball ☐ harder than
☐ harder than   the other boys in his
☐ more hard than

team and he can run ☐ most fastly.
☐ most fast.
☐ the fastest.

In an a_____ (= usual, normal) match
he usually scores three goals.

Yesterday, however, he played ☐ worse than
☐ more bad than   before.
☐ bader than

He was _____ (= sth that is easy to see) in a bad _____

(= the way you feel) because his coach wanted him to play ☐ different.
☐ differently.

He doesn't like any kind of _____ (verb: to criticize → noun) and always

wants to be perfect. In the middle of the match he c_____ a foul and spoke

rather _____ (≠ friendly) to the _____ on the

p_____ (= field). When the other team scored a p_____y,

he complained _____ (= at once, directly). After the match he

d_____ (= he went away) very ☐ quick   and I met him in the changing
☐ quickly

room, where nobody wanted to talk to him or _____ (= to interrupt) him.

He was very thirsty, but he didn't have a bottle, so I gave him ~~my bottle~~ _____ .

Of course he didn't thank me.

In the evening, his sister tried to cheer him up and _____ (= turned) on the

radio. Unfortunately, the song that was played sounded very ☐ sad.
☐ sadly.

So he still felt very ☐ bad   and looked ☐ unhappy.
☐ badly   ☐ unhappily.

Schulaufgabe 4

Workshop 2
→ students' book, pp. 58/59

He even didn't like his sandwich, which _____ (= *definitely*) tasted ☐ delicious, ☐ deliciously, so his sister gave him ~~her sandwich~~ _____ . But he was still hungry and before his parents could eat their sandwiches, he even ate ~~their sandwich~~ _____ , too. At 10 o'clock he f_____ly went to bed. His sister didn't want to wake him up again, so she walked past his door very ☐ slow, ☐ slowly, and closed the door to her room as ☐ careful ☐ carfuly ☐ carfully as she could. You see, James actually can be quite complicated.

›› 2 Use of English: A footballer from Hill End School (Fast Track)

Mixed Bag (30 CP)

_____ → Please fill in the missing word(s).
~~my book~~ → Please use a possessive pronoun to replace the expression.
.... → Please fill in one of the following adjectives in the correct form.
 Be careful: adjective or adverb?
 Sometimes you need the comparative or superlative.

> bad ■ different ■ early ■ fast ■ hard ■ quick

James is one of the best football players at Hill End School. He started his career .... his friends. He can kick the ball .... the other boys in his team and he can run .... In an _____ (= *usual, normal*) match he usually scores three goals. Yesterday, however, he played .... before. He was _____ (= *sth that is easy to see*) in a bad _____ (= *the way you are feeling*) because the coach wanted him to play .... He doesn't like any kind of _____ (verb: *to criticize* → *noun*) and always wants to be perfect. In the middle of the match he c_____ a foul and spoke rather _____ (≠ *friendly*) to the _____ on the _____ (= *field*). When the other team scored a goal from a p_____y , he complained _____ (= *at once, directly*).

Schulaufgabe 4 — Workshop 2

→ students' book, pp. 60/63

After the match he _____ (= *he went away*) very ....

and I met him in the changing room, where nobody wanted to talk to him or

_____ (= *to interrupt*) him. He was very thirsty, but he didn't have a

bottle, so I gave him ~~my bottle~~ _____ . Of course he didn't thank me.

> bad ■ careful ■ delicious ■ sad ■ slow ■ unhappy

In the evening, his sister tried to cheer him up and _____ (= *turned*)

on the radio. Unfortunately, the song which they could hear sounded very

.... So he still felt very .... and

looked .... He even didn't like his sandwich, which

_____ (= *definitely*) tasted .... so his

sister gave him ~~her sandwich~~ _____ . But he was still hungry and before his parents

could eat their sandwiches, he even ate ~~their sandwich~~ _____ , too.

At 10 o'clock he f_____ly went to bed. His sister didn't want to wake him up

again, so she walked past his door very .... and closed the door to

her room as .... as she could. You see, James actually can be quite

complicated.

3 Mediation: Die Bretter, die die Welt bedeuten (30 CP)

Du nimmst während der Ferien an einem internationalen Jugendtheaterworkshop in München teil, bei dem Jugendliche aus ganz Europa gemeinsam eine englischsprachige Theateraufführung vorbereiten und durchführen. Nach den Einführungsveranstaltungen der ersten Woche musst du ein Auswahlverfahren bestehen, bei dem eine Jury entscheidet, ob du weiter mitmachen darfst und welche Aufgabe zu deinen Fähigkeiten passt.

In der Jury sitzt Matthias O., ein berühmter deutscher Schauspieler. Um dich bestmöglich auf sein Urteil vorzubereiten, hast du ein Interview mit ihm im Internet gelesen. Natürlich möchtest du gerne gemeinsam mit deinen neuen Freunden aus Frankreich, Dänemark und Italien, die du bei diesem Workshop kennengelernt hast, in die nächste Runde kommen, und erklärst ihnen deshalb, worauf Matthias O. Wert legt. Da sie kaum Deutsch sprechen, beantwortest du ihre Fragen auf Englisch.

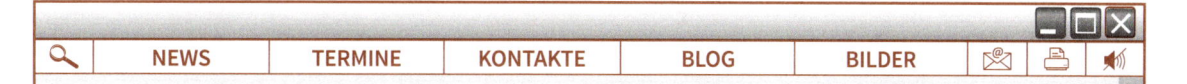

Matthias O. sucht Münchens nächste Filmstars

Wer träumt nicht davon, eines Tages der Newcomer der großen Online-Streaming-Dienste zu werden? Den Absolventen des internationalen Jugendtheaterworkshops, der momentan in München stattfindet, werden viele Möglichkeiten offenstehen. Shootingstar Matthias O. hat uns in einem Exklusiv-Interview verraten, was die Teilnehmer brauchen, um in die zweite Runde zu kommen.

Viele Jugendliche träumen von einer großen Karriere als Schauspieler. Sie wollen im Rahmen ihres Jugendworkshops ein Trittbrett bieten, das es talentierten Jugendlichen ermöglicht, in der Schauspielbranche Fuß zu fassen. Warum haben Sie sich dafür eingesetzt, dass alle angebotenen Veranstaltungen auf Englisch stattfinden?

Matthias O.: Wer als Schauspieler international Erfolg haben will, muss fließend Englisch sprechen, und zwar nicht nur, um in Hollywood bestehen zu können. Weltweit finden nämlich die meisten Castings auf Englisch statt, weshalb wir auch hier nur Jugendliche in die nächste Runde vorrücken lassen, die während der ersten Woche gezeigt haben, dass sie sehr gut Englisch sprechen – und zwar nicht nur bei auswendig gelernten Theaterstücken.

Wie wird das Auswahlverfahren, das Sie eben angesprochen haben, ablaufen?

Matthias O.: Im Rahmen des Auswahlverfahrens müssen alle Jungschauspieler eine schwierige Textpassage in kurzer Zeit auswendig lernen und dann möglichst überzeugend vortragen. Dabei zeigt sich sehr schnell, wer ein gutes Gedächtnis hat und wer dazu neigt, in der Nervosität seinen Text zu vergessen oder die Nerven zu verlieren.

Haben denn nur schauspielbegeisterte Jugendliche die Möglichkeit, in diesem Jugendtheaterworkshop den Grundstein für eine vielversprechende Karriere zu legen?

Matthias O.: Nein, natürlich nicht. Denn selbst wenn die Schauspieler vordergründig im Rampenlicht stehen, kann keine Aufführung stattfinden, wenn nicht zahlreiche fleißige Hände im Hintergrund die Fäden ziehen. Alle diejenigen, die lieber hinter der Bühne stehen wollen, können sich in verschiedenen Gruppen als Maskenbildner, Kostümdesigner, Tonspezialisten, Lichttechniker oder Bühnengestalter spezialisieren. Wer bereits Nähkenntnisse besitzt, kann gemeinsam mit unseren Schneidermeistern aufregende Roben kreieren. Technikbegeisterte Teilnehmer kümmern sich darum, dass die Schauspieler immer im Rampenlicht stehen und gut zu verstehen sind, während künstlerisch und handwerklich begabte Jugendliche aufwendige Bühnenbilder und Requisiten herstellen können.

Sind das also Jobs für diejenigen, die sich vor dem Text drücken wollen?

Matthias O.: Nein, ganz und gar nicht, denn natürlich müssen diejenigen, die sich diesen Aufgaben widmen, auch eine hervorragende Textkenntnis besitzen. Nur so können sie die notwendige Stimmung mit den richtigen Licht- und Soundeffekten verstärken oder immer adäquat auf den nächsten Szenenwechsel vorbereitet sein.

Schulaufgabe 4 — Workshop 2

→ students' book, pp. 60-63

> *Aber dennoch handelt es sich dabei um weniger angesehene Aufgaben, oder?*
>
> **Matthias O.:** Das sehe ich anders, denn insbesondere die Tontechniker haben einen großen Einfluss auf den Erfolg des Stückes, der maßgeblich vom Eindruck der Zuschauer abhängt. Fühlen sich diese wegen der viel zu lauten Musik unwohl oder können sie die Dialoge kaum verstehen, werden sie unzufrieden nach Hause gehen und uns in den Online-Rezensionen nicht gut dastehen lassen. Da können die Schauspieler noch so talentiert sein – ohne ein gutes Team haben sie kaum eine Chance auf Erfolg. Deshalb legen wir auch großen Wert darauf, dass diejenigen Teilnehmer, die in die nächste Runde kommen, keine Einzelkämpfer sind, sondern beweisen, dass sie kollegial mit ihren Mitstreitern zusammenarbeiten können.

Alessandro: Can you tell us more about the challenges of the next competition?

You: _____

Julie: What's important for Matthias?

You: _____

Malte: I didn't remember my lines in the last rehearsal and I'm sure that I won't succeed. Is there any alternative for me if I don't want to be an actor?

You: _____

Schulaufgabe 4 — Workshop 2

→ students' book, pp. 60-63

Pierre So you can go on even if you don't know the script?!

You _____

_____

_____

_____

_____

_____

Pierre But these jobs are much less important, I'm sure he thinks so, too!

You _____

_____

_____

_____

_____

_____

_____

Anyway, I'm sure we're on the right track since we're a good English-speaking team with different abilities. Let's keep our fingers crossed[1] for the challenge …

---

[1] **fingers crossed** You do this when you want to wish somebody good luck

Schulaufgabe 5 (80 CP)

1 Reading comprehension: The Afanc (20 CP)

Read the texts, then do the tasks.

From: Bex
To: Deepak
Subject: The Afanc

Hi Deepak,

I hope you are okay. Did you like my report on our visit to Chirk Castle? I forgot to tell you that there are a lot of mysterious stories in Wales. Some people have even seen ghosts at the castle! On the Internet I have found another creepy story about Wales – thank God it's about the North of Wales … It's called "The Legend of the River Conwy Afanc". Now read this:

The legend says that there was a period in time when the people who lived along the Conwy Valley on the northern Welsh coast were constantly disturbed by terrible floods that both ruined their fields and killed their animals. Everybody knew that the floods were caused by the Afanc. The Afanc was a legendary Welsh water monster, maybe a little bit like the Scottish Loch Ness monster. People say it looked like a mixture between a crocodile, a huge beaver and a dinosaur. Can you imagine?

The Afanc lived in Llyn-yr-Afanc in the River Conwy. It was a gigantic beast who, when somebody annoyed it, was strong enough to break the banks[1] of the lake causing the floods. Also, everybody who swam in its lake was eaten immediately – skin, clothes, shoes, bones, everything. The people of the village tried their very best to kill him but it seems that his skin was so thick and strong that no spear, arrow or any weapon could pierce it.

The wise men of the valley held a meeting and decided that if nothing else worked, then they would have to lead the Afanc out of his lake and move him to a lake far away across the mountains, where he could cause no further trouble. The lake that was chosen to be the Afanc's new home was Llyn Ffynnon Las, under the dark shadow of Mount Snowdon. That's where Snowdonia National Park is, you know?

Preparations started straight away: the best blacksmith[2] in the land made strong iron chains that they needed to bind and secure the Afanc, and they sent for a man called Hu Gardan and his two long-horned oxen – the strongest oxen in Wales – to come and help them with their mission.

But there was a big problem: The Afanc decided not to come out of his pool. However, it appears that the Afanc, like many other ugly old monsters, was very fond of beautiful young women, and one girl in particular, the daughter of a local farmer, was brave enough to help the villagers.

The girl went towards the Afanc's lake while her father and the rest of the men were hiding a short distance away. While she was standing on the shore and calling him in a soft and friendly voice, the waters began to open up and soon everybody could see the huge head of the monster.

---

[1] **bank** the border of a lake or river
[2] **blacksmith** someone who produces metal tools or weapons

Schulaufgabe 5 — Workshop 3

→ students' book, p. 81

Although the girl was quite scared, which I can perfectly understand, she didn't run away but looked fearlessly into the monster's green-black eyes and began to sing a traditional, soft Welsh song. Slowly the massive great body of the Afanc moved out of the lake towards the girl. So sweet was the song that the Afanc's head slowly sank to the ground and he fell asleep on the girl's legs. The girl waved to her father, and he and the rest of the men came out from their hiding places and started to put the Afanc in chains.

They had only just finished their task when the Afanc awoke, and with a roar[1], the monster slid back into the lake. Fortunately, the chains were long and the oxen braced their muscles and began to pull. Slowly, the Afanc was pulled out of the water, but it was very very hard work.

They pulled him up the Lledr valley, and then headed north-west toward Llyn Ffynnon Las. On the way up a steep mountain one of the oxen was pulling so hard that it lost an eye. The tears the oxen cried formed Pwll Llygad yr Ych, which means "Pool of the Ox's Eye".

The mighty oxen struggled on until they reached Llyn Ffynnon Las, close to the top of Snowdon. There the chains of the Afanc were removed, and with a roar, the monster jumped straight into the deep blue water that was his new home from then on. He wasn't able to break out any more because of the many stones around the lake. (That's what they believe….)

But Deepak, some legends say it ended differently! One says that the Afanc didn't reach any other lake but is still living inside a cave. And there are many many caves in Wales! Believe me, I am surely not going inside any cave here in Wales!
Well, I hope you like this little legend. I don't, actually.

More later!
Bex

---

1 Right or wrong? Tick (✓) the correct answers and correct the false statements. (8 CP)

	right	wrong
1 The Afanc is a scary ghost.	☐	☐
2 The actions of the Afanc were a big problem for the farmers of Conwy valley.	☐	☐
3 When the farmers tried to kill the Afanc, he came out and ate them alive.	☐	☐
4 The Afanc is very similar to Nessie, the Scottish monster.	☐	☐
5 The Afanc was very brutal and killed people for no reason.	☐	☐

---

[1] **roar** a very loud and frightening sound

Schulaufgabe 5 — Workshop 3
→ students' book, p. 81

2 Tick (✓) the correct answers. Only one answer is correct. (4 CP)

1 The people of the valley decided to…
☐ buy more arrows and spears from a better blacksmith.
☐ move the Afanc into a cave.
☐ throw a beautiful girl into the water to feed him.
☐ move the Afanc onto the other side of Mount Snowdon.

2 When the Afanc didn't come out of the lake, the people…
☐ didn't know what to do.
☐ invited Hu Gardan to help them.
☐ needed a beautiful girl who could help them.
☐ were frustrated and gave up.

3 The Afanc…
☐ heard the beautiful girl sing and jumped out of the lake.
☐ heard the iron chains and was afraid.
☐ heard the girl sing and slowly came out of the lake.
☐ attacked the girl because he didn't like her singing.

4 It was quite difficult…
☐ for the oxen to pull the Afanc out of the water.
☐ for the girl to remember her song.
☐ for the blacksmith to concentrate.
☐ for the oxen to swim.

3 Complete the statements. (4 CP)

1 When the Afanc realized that the people of the valley wanted to pull him out of his lake, he
_____
_____

2 In North Wales, there is a lake called 'Pool of the Ox's Eye' because _____
_____

4 Answer the questions in complete sentences. (4 CP)

1 Why did the people believe that they were safe in the end?
_____
_____

2 Why does Bex say in the end that she is not going to visit any more caves in Wales?
_____
_____

Schulaufgabe 5 — Workshop 3
→ students' book, pp. 78–85

2 Use of English: A trip to Llangollen (On Track)
Mixed Bag (30 CP)

Fill the gaps with

_____ → reflexive or reciprocal pronouns

---------- → nouns, adjectives or adverbs

.... → the correct form of the verb in brackets. In some gaps, you needn't write anything. Cross these gaps out.

'Let's visit LLangollen!'

David and his Dad are planning their day in Llangollen.

David So, Dad, what .... (we / do) in Llangollen?

Mr Sinclair Well, there are many ---------------- (≠ far away) attractions we can visit. I am very interested in the Llangollen Motor Museum. Its website says that we can see more than sixty vehicles, and some of them are still drivable. Most of the cars and motorcycles are really o---------f---------- (≠ modern), too – from my ---------------------- (= time before you grow up)! I remember how I .... (have) a motorcycle accident when I was a young man.

David .... (you / hurt) _____ ?

Mr. Sinclair Yes, unfortunately, I .... (break) my left leg. I .... (not / drive) very ---------------- (= carefully).

David Oh, you .... (never / tell) me!

Mr Sinclair I know, I .... (to be ashamed) of _____ .

David That's nothing to be ashamed of, Dad.

Mr Sinclair Well, it's a long time ago. Let's not worry _____ about the past. Let's talk about the future! Maybe .... (we / travel) on the Llangollen Railway. The journey is a relaxing ten miles and goes through the stunning Dee Valley to the lovely town of Corwen in North Wales. I .... (always / want) to travel on a p---------------- (≠ exciting) historic train, which transported ---------------- such as food and coal in the past. OK, but I'm sure you .... (be bored) after only a few minutes.

Schulaufgabe 5

Workshop 3
→ students' book, page 78 – 85

David   That's not true! I .... (just / need) some snacks.

Mr Sinclair All right, let's concentrate _____ on our plans. The Llangollen Railway website also says that visitors .... (enjoy) stunning views over the Dee valley.

David   But that .... (sound) _ _ _ _ _ _ _ _ _ _ _ _ _ _ _ _ (= absolutely) boring!

Mr Sinclair Why? I .... (think) you were interested in trains!

David   But Dad! I .... (not / be) five years anymore! You .... (just / mention) the River Dee: What about wild water rafting?

Mr Sinclair That's actually not a bad idea. Let me see – the website says that the staff .... (give) us all the equipment we need.

David   And we can help _____ with the wetsuits!

Mr Sinclair OK then, the afternoon trip .... (start) at 1.30 pm. It'll be fun!

>>> 2 Use of English: A trip to Llangollen (Fast Track)

Mixed Bag (30 CP)

Fill the gaps with

_____   → reflexive or reciprocal pronouns

- - - - - - -   → nouns, adjectives or adverbs

.... → one of the verbs from the box in the correct form (X = negative form).

In some gaps, you needn't write anything. Cross these gaps out. You can use the verbs more than once.

> be ashamed ■ break ■ be bored ■ do ■ drive ■ enjoy ■ give ■ hurt ■ mention
> ■ start ■ sound ■ tell ■ think ■ travel / ride ■ want

'Let's visit LLangollen!'

David and his Dad are planning their day in Llangollen.

David   So, Dad, what .... (we) in Llangollen?

Mr Sinclair Well, there are many - - - - - - - - - - - - - - - - - - (≠ far away) attractions we can visit. I am very interested in the Llangollen Motor Museum. Its

Schulaufgabe 5

Workshop 3
→ students' book, pp. 78–85

website says that we can see more than sixty vehicles, and some of them are still drivable. Most of the cars and motorcycles are really o_ _ _ _ _ _ _ _-f_ _ _ _ _ _ _ _ (≠ modern), too – from my _ _ _ _ _ _ _ _ _ _ _ _ _ _ _ _ _ _ (= time before you grow up)! I remember how I _ _ _ _ _ _ _ _ _ _ a motorcycle accident when I was a young man.

David _ _ _ _ _ _ _ _ _ _ _ _ _ _ _ (you) _ _ _ _ _ _ _ _ _ _ ?

Mr. Sinclair Yes, unfortunately, I _ _ _ _ _ _ _ _ _ _ _ _ _ _ my left leg. I _ _ _ _ _ _ _ _ _ _ _ _ _ _ _ (X) very _ _ _ _ _ _ _ _ _ _ _ _ _ _ _ _ (= carefully).

David Oh, you _ _ _ _ _ _ _ _ _ _ _ _ _ _ (never) me!

Mr Sinclair I know, I _ _ _ _ _ _ _ _ _ _ _ _ _ _ of _ _ _ _ _ _ _ _ _ _ _ _ .

David That's nothing to be ashamed of, Dad.

Mr Sinclair Yes, but it's a long time ago. Let's not worry _ _ _ _ _ _ _ _ _ _ _ _ _ _ _ about the past. Let's talk about the future! Maybe _ _ _ _ _ _ _ _ _ _ _ _ _ _ _ _ _ (we) on the Llangollen Railway. The journey is a relaxing ten miles travelling through the stunning Dee Valley to the lovely town of Corwen in North Wales. I _ _ _ _ _ _ _ _ _ _ _ _ _ _ _ _ _ _ (always) to travel on a p_ _ _ _ _ _ _ _ _ _ _ _ _ _ _ _ (≠ exciting) historic train, which transported _ _ _ _ _ _ _ _ _ _ _ _ _ _ _ _ _ _ such as food and coal in the past. Ok, but I'm sure you _ _ _ _ _ _ _ _ _ _ _ _ _ _ _ _ after only a few minutes.

David That's not true! I _ _ _ _ _ _ _ _ _ _ _ _ _ _ _ _ _ _ (just) some snacks.

Mr Sinclair All right, let's concentrate _ _ _ _ _ _ _ _ _ _ _ _ _ _ _ _ on our plans. The Llangollen Railway website also says that visitors _ _ _ _ _ _ _ _ _ _ _ _ _ _ _ _ stunning views over the Dee valley.

David But that _ (= absolutely) boring!

Mr Sinclair Why? I _ _ _ _ _ _ _ _ _ _ _ _ _ _ _ you were interested in trains!

David But Dad! I _ _ _ _ _ _ _ _ _ _ _ _ _ _ _ (X) five years anymore! You _ _ _ _ _ _ _ _ _ _ _ _ _ _ _ _ _ _ the River Dee: What about wild water rafting?

Mr Sinclair That's actually not a bad idea. Let me see – the website says that the staff _ _ _ _ _ _ _ _ _ _ _ _ _ _ _ _ us all the equipment we need.

David And we can help _ _ _ _ _ _ _ _ _ _ _ _ _ _ _ with the wetsuits!

Mr Sinclair OK then, the afternoon trip _ _ _ _ _ _ _ _ _ _ _ _ _ _ _ at 1.30 pm. It'll be fun!

3 Writing: A holiday in Wales (30 CP)

You're spending two weeks of your summer holidays in Wales with your family. It's the end of the first week and you're writing an email to an English friend to tell him or her about your holiday.

Write about all of these aspects:
- how you got there
- where you are staying
- how the weather, the people, the food are
- two activities of the first week
- your plans for the second week

Write about 120 words on an extra sheet.

Schulaufgabe 6

Workshop 3
→ students' book, complete workshop 3

@ SNG-40893-003

Schulaufgabe 6 (86 CP)

1 Listening comprehension: The Red Lion (20 CP)

1 Right or wrong? Listen, then tick (✓) the correct answers and correct the false statements. (8 CP)

		right	wrong
1	David found a website about pubs along the canal, with information on the nearest lock and the mooring prices.	☐	☐
2	Mr Sinclair likes the website.	☐	☐
3	Mr Sinclair read an article on pub names on the internet.	☐	☐
4	In the UK there are over 700 pubs with the name 'The Red Lion'.	☐	☐
5	David believes that many pubs in Wales are called 'The Red Lion'.	☐	☐

2 Tick the correct answers. Only one answer is correct. (3 CP)

1 Mr Sinclair explains that…
a the name 'Red Lion' is thousands of years old. ☐
b it was used by King John. ☐
c it was used as a symbol of power. ☐
d it was used on a flag. ☐

2 Mr Sinclair informs David that…
a the original red lion died in the 13th century. ☐
b John of Gaunt lived until 1399. ☐
c two of John of Gaunt's knights died in 1399. ☐
d the red lion died one night in the 14th century. ☐

3 One of the pub classics served in 'The Red Lion' is…
a pork chops with gravy and mashed potatoes. ☐
b pork sausages with black pudding and roast vegetables. ☐
c pasta with mushrooms, garden peas and salad. ☐
d pork sausages with black pudding and mashed potatoes. ☐

3 Complete the statements. (3 CP)

Mr Sinclair   But David, ham is not exactly vegetarian …

David   Oh, yes, that's _____. But you needn't be so

_____ ! Anyway, she can order a salad – there are plenty of

salad dishes on the menu, too! I'm sure she's going to have the one

© Westermann Gruppe

Schulaufgabe 6 Workshop **3**
→ students' book, complete workshop 3

with roast vegetables. And just look at the list of desserts! You can't _____ about that! Desserts are mainly vegetarian, aren't they, Dad?

4 **Answer the questions in complete sentences.** (4 CP)

1 Why is David going to call the pub?
_____
_____

2 Why is Mr Sinclair worried at the end?
_____
_____

2 Use of English: Famous Welshmen and Welshwomen (On Track)

Mixed tenses (24 CP)

Bex's homework is to make a poster about 'Five Famous People from Wales'. She has already found some information on the internet and is now talking to her mum about it. Fill in the gaps with the right form of the verbs in brackets.

'Five Famous People from Wales'

Mrs Sinclair So, Bex, have you got much homework?

Bex It's ok. I _____ (make) poster about 'Five Famous People from Wales' at the moment.

Mrs Sinclair And _____ (find / you / already) any information you can use?

Bex Yes, I have! The oldest famous Welsh person I found is King Arthur. Before he managed to pull a sword out of a stone and became the new king, there _____ (be) many battles with the country's enemies.

Mrs Sinclair When did King Arthur live?

Bex I don't know exactly when he _____ (live). But I'm sure that he _____ (die) before my next famous Welsh person was born. His name is Thomas Myddelton.

Mrs Sinclair Isn't this the one who lived in Chirk Castle?

Schulaufgabe 6 — Workshop 3

→ students' book, complete workshop 3

Bex   That's right. Before Thomas Myddelton _____ (buy) Chirk Castle in 1595, he _____ (work) as a grocer in London. Until he _____ (make) a lot of money from the East India Company, he had not been very rich. His family lived in the Castle for more than 300 years.

Mrs Sinclair   Does the family still live there today?

Bex   I don't know! Anyway, our next person is very famous, too!

Mrs. Sinclair   Who are you talking about?

Bex   I _____ (talk) about George Everest. Sir George Everest.

Mrs Sinclair   Everest? Like the world's highest mountain?

Bex   Exactly. Sir George Everest _____ (be) a famous Welsh person who lived in the 18th century. Before his family moved to London, he _____ (spend) his childhood in Wales. It is not even clear whether he was born in Wales, but his family had owned a house there before they _____ (go) to London.

Mrs Sinclair   That's interesting! I didn't know that!

Bex   As you said before, Mum, the world's highest mountain – Mount Everest – was named after him, but Everest's name was a compromise[1] because the Indian people _____ (already use) many different names for the mountain.

Mrs Sinclair   So Mr Everest was really proud that they wanted to use his name for the mountain, wasn't he?

Bex   No, not really! Sir George _____ (not like) the idea at first as he _____ (have) nothing to do with the discovery of the mountain and he _____ (think) his name was difficult to pronounce and write in the Hindi language.

Mrs Sinclair   Oh, I see. So, who is your next famous person?

Bex   It's a boxer called Jimmy Wilde. It was Dad's idea. You know, he is a great fan of boxing and he _____ (know) everything about Welsh sports. Jimmy Wilde was born in Cardiff, which had always been the industrial centre of Wales. Dad told me that before Wilde _____ (become) the world lightweight champion in 1923, he _____ (fight) in hundreds of fights. _____ (you / ever / hear) of him?

---

[1] **compromise** when you come to an agreement with someone

Schulaufgabe 6 — Workshop 3

→ students' book, complete workshop 3

Mrs Sinclair No, I haven't, actually. I'm not interested in sports. I'm more interested in music.

Bex Great! Then you _____ (like) my fifth famous Welsh person!

Mrs Sinclair Is it an actress? Is it Catherine Zeta-Jones, for example?

Bex No, it's a singer and songwriter! Our last famous Welsh person is Duffy. Did you know that she was very unhappy when her family moved to England because she _____ (not want) to leave Wales? Just like Everest! Until her family moved to England, Duffy _____ (never speak) English, but Welsh! She said that it had been really hard to learn it until she made some English-speaking friends at her new school.

Mrs Sinclair Oh, poor girl!

Bex Yes, I agree. That's why I must go now and _____ (meet) some of my own English-speaking friends.

Use of English: Vocabulary (12 CP)

Now meet David and his geography teacher, Mr Summers. David hasn't done his homework. Choose suitable adjectives and adverbs to complete the dialogue.

Mr Summers So David, you haven't done your homework again! I'm really co_____!

David I'm sorry, Mr Summers. I couldn't do it yesterday because I was cleaning the floor in the kitchen and then it was wet and sl_____ and I fell down. I had an accident!

Mr Summers I see. So you are not an ex_____ cleaner?

David No, I'm not. And after I had fallen down I was feeling di_____, too, and my face turned very pa_____.

Mr Summers David, I am really re_____ that you were able to come to school today!

David Yes, I know, Mr Summers, you are really not am_____. But I was absolutely te_____ because I thought I had to go to hospital!

Mr Summers But David, don't be so fr_____! I'm actually am_____ about your imagination!

Schulaufgabe 6   Workshop 3
→ students' book, complete workshop 3

David   Well, I'm sorry, Mr Summers, don't be an_____ with me. I promise to be more am_____ with my homework next time!

2 Use of English: Famous Welshmen and Welshwomen (Fast Track)
Mixed tenses (24 CP)

Bex's homework is to make a poster about 'Five Famous People from Wales'. She has already found some information on the internet and is now talking to her mum about it.

Fill in the gaps with the right form of one of the verbs below. You can use the verbs more than once.

'Five Famous People from Wales'

> be ■ buy ■ die ■ find ■ go ■ live ■ make ■ spend ■ talk ■ work

Mrs Sinclair   So, Bex, have you got much homework?

Bex   It's ok. I _____ a poster about 'Five Famous People from Wales' at the moment.

Mrs. Sinclair   And _____ (already / you) any information you can use?

Bex   Yes, I have! The oldest famous Welsh person I have found is King Arthur. Before he managed to pull a sword out of a stone and became the new king, there _____ many battles with the country's enemies.

Mrs Sinclair   When did King Arthur live?

Bex   I don't know exactly when he _____ . But I'm sure that he _____ before my next famous Welsh person was born. His name is Thomas Myddelton.

Mrs Sinclair   Isn't this the one who lived in Chirk Castle?

Bex   That's right. Before Thomas Myddelton _____ Chirk Castle in 1595, he _____ as a grocer in London. Until he _____ a lot of money from the East India Company, he had not been very rich. His family lived in the Castle for more than 300 years.

Mrs Sinclair   Do the family still live there today?

Bex   I don't know! Anyway, our next person is very famous, too!

© Westermann Gruppe

Schulaufgabe 6 — Workshop 3

→ students' book, workshop 3

Mrs. Sinclair Who are you talking about?

Bex I _____ about George Everest. Sir George Everest.

Mrs. Sinclair Everest? Like the world's highest mountain?

Bex Exactly. Sir George Everest _____ a famous Welsh person who lived in the 18th century. Before his family moved to London, he _____ his childhood in Wales. It is not even really sure that he was born in Wales, but his family had owned a house there before they _____ to London.

> become ■ fight ■ have ■ hear ■ know ■ like ■ meet ■ speak ■ think ■ use ■ want

Mrs Sinclair That's interesting! I didn't know this!

Bex As you said before, Mum, the world's highest mountain – Mount Everest – was named after him, but Everest's name was a compromise because the Indian people _____ (already) many different names for the mountain.

Mrs Sinclair So Mr Everest was really proud that they wanted to use his name for the mountain, wasn't he?

Bex No, not really! Sir George _____ (not) the idea at first as he _____ nothing to do with the discovery of the mountain and he _____ his name was difficult to pronounce and write in the Hindi language.

Mrs Sinclair Oh, I see. So, who is your next famous person?

Bex It's a boxer called Jimmy Wilde. It was Dad's idea. You know, he is a great fan of boxing and he _____ everything about Welsh sports. Jimmy Wilde was born in Cardiff, which had always been the industrial centre of Wales. Dad told me that before Wilde _____ the world lightweight champion in 1923, he _____ in hundreds of fights. _____ (you / ever) of him?

Mrs Sinclair No, I haven't, actually. I'm not interested in sports. I'm more interested in popular culture.

Bex What's that?

Mrs Sinclair That's modern entertainment, like television, films, and music!

Bex Great! Then you _____ my fifth famous Welsh person!

Schulaufgabe 6 — Workshop 3

→ students' book, workshop 3

Mrs Sinclair	Is it an actress? Is it Catherine Zeta-Jones, for example?
Bex	No, it's a singer and songwriter! Our last famous Welsh person is Duffy. Did you know that she was very unhappy when her family moved to England because she _____ (not) to leave Wales? Just like Everest! Until her family moved to England, Duffy _____ (never) English, but Welsh! She said that it had been really hard to learn it until she made some English-speaking friends at her new school.
Mrs Sinclair	Oh, poor girl!
Bex	Yes, I agree. That's why I must go now and _____ some of my own English-speaking friends.

2 Use of English: Vocabulary (12 CP)

Now meet David and his geography teacher, Mr Summers. David hasn't done his homework. Choose adjectives and adverbs to complete the dialogue. You don't need all of the words!

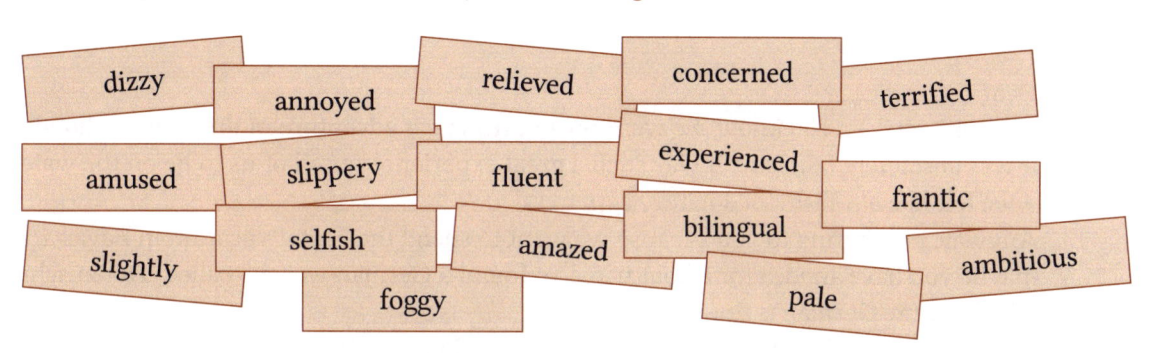

dizzy · annoyed · relieved · concerned · terrified · amused · slippery · fluent · experienced · frantic · slightly · selfish · amazed · bilingual · ambitious · foggy · pale

Mr Summers	So David, you haven't done your homework again! I'm really _____!
David	I'm sorry, Mr Summers. I couldn't do it yesterday because I was cleaning the floor in the kitchen and then it was wet and _____ and I fell down. I had an accident!
Mr Summers	I see. So you are not an _____ cleaner?
David	No, I'm not. And after I had fallen down I was feeling _____, too, and my face turned very _____.
Mr Summers	David, I am really _____ that you were able to come to school today!
David	Yes, I know, Mr Summers, you are really not _____. But I was absolutely _____ because I thought I had to go to hospital!

Schulaufgabe 6 — Workshop 3

→ students' book, pp. 100/101

Mr Summers But David, don't be so _____ ! I'm actually

_____ about your imagination!

David Well, I'm sorry, Mr Summers, don't be _____ with me.

I promise to be more _____ with my homework next time!

M 3 Mediation: Osterferien in Bayern (30 CP)

Die Sinclairs (Mr and Mrs Sinclair, David und Bex) haben Gefallen an Urlaub auf dem Wasser gefunden, seitdem sie in Wales mit dem Narrowboat *Firefly* unterwegs waren. In diesem Jahr möchten sie aber die Osterferien in Bayern verbringen. Sie fragen dich, ob du eine interessante Idee für einen wasserbezogenen Ausflug hättest. Du findest eine passende Website (S. 53).

Lies Davids E-Mail und die Informationen auf der Website und beantworte seine Fragen in deiner Antwortmail. Schreibe deine E-Mail auf ein separates Blatt (Umfang: ca. 120 Wörter).

To: David
From: _____
Subject: Our trip to Bavaria

Dear _____ ,

How are you? As you know, we went on a narrowboat adventure in the summer holidays. It was absolutely fantastic. It was such a great experience for all of us to be on the water – we felt like old-fashioned nature explorers!

Anyway, I'm writing to you because we want to spend the Easter vacation in Bavaria, and maybe you have an idea for a boat trip. I've found a German website called 'Donauschifffahrt' but my German is not very good.

Is there a way to do some sightseeing by boat? What does the website say about 'Regensburg' – is this an interesting city? What are the prices for the boat trip? Can we eat on the boat? Can we bring our dog Coco, too?

Thank you for your help!

David

| NEWS | TERMINE | KONTAKTE | BLOG | BILDER |

Historische Strudelrundfahrt in Regensburg

Sightseeing an Bord der historischen MS Bruckmadl

Ein Hauch von Geschichte weht mit dem Fahrtwind um die Nase! An Bord der MS Bruckmadl erfahren die Fahrgäste bei der „Historischen Strudelrundfahrt" nicht nur viel von der reichhaltigen Geschichte Regensburgs. Diese Schifffahrt ist auch eine Reise in die Vergangenheit der Binnenschifffahrt, denn das Bruckmadl war unter dem Namen MS Agnes Bernauer seit Beginn mit dabei. Heute strahlt es zwar in modernen, lässig-maritimen Style, hat aber nichts von seinem historischen Charme verloren.

Das Hauptaugenmerk der Rundfahrt selbst liegt auf der Geschichte von Regensburg, Wissens- und Sehenswertes wird bei der 45-minütigen Fahrt unter der Steinernen Brücke hindurch per Bordlautsprecher erläutert. Ein Muss für Touristen wie Einheimische!

Regensburg ist mit über 150.000 Einwohnern die viertgrößte Stadt Bayerns. Die exponierte Lage an vier Flüssen brachte der Stadt Regensburg auch früher schon eine außergewöhnliche wirtschaftsstrategische Position ein. Ein Spaziergang durch die historische Altstadt ist der beste Weg, um die Schönheit der mittelalterlichen Stadt kennenzulernen. Die Altstadt in Stadtamhof wurde 2006 sogar mit dem Titel UNESCO-Welterbe ausgezeichnet. Entdecken Sie den gotischen Regensburger Dom Sankt Peter, das Alte Rathaus, die Steinerne Brücke, die Porta Praetoria u. v. m. Unsere Anlegestelle befindet sich an der Historischen Wurstkuchl Nr. 1 (der ältesten Bratwurststube der Welt), direkt an der Steinernen Brücke.

Termine
6 x täglich von 20. April bis 6. Oktober
Vorsaison: jeweils am Samstag und Sonntag von 06. bis 14. April
Nachsaison: jeweils am Samstag und Sonntag von 12. bis 27. Oktober
und täglich von 28. Oktober bis 03. November

Fahrzeiten
Abfahrten um 10:30 Uhr, 11:30 Uhr, 12:30 Uhr, 13:30 Uhr, 14:30 Uhr und 15:30 Uhr
Fahrtdauer ca. 45 Minuten

Fahrpreis
9,50 € pro Person
Kinder (6 bis einschl. 13 Jahre) 50 % Ermäßigung, Kinder bis 5 Jahre frei

Speisenangebot
Getränke und Snacks an Bord erhältlich: Heiße Getränke, Bier, nichtalkoholische Getränke, kleine Gerichte, verschiedene frische Kuchen und Eis

Hunde an Bord erlaubt. Bitte an die Leine nehmen.

Schulaufgabe 7 (84 CP)

1 Listening comprehension: Welcome to Denver, Colorado! (24 CP)

Listen carefully to the radio report and complete the tasks below.

1 Right or wrong? Tick the correct answers and correct the false statements. (8 CP)

		right	wrong
1	The capital of Colorado is Denver.	☐	☐
2	Denver is called 'mile high city' because it's just one mile away from the Rocky Mountains.	☐	☐
3	Arizona is the largest city in the US West because 700,000 people live there.	☐	☐
4	Altogether, there are three swimming pools at the Recreation Centre.	☐	☐
5	Inside the gymnasium, you can play volleyball, basketball and climb up a climbing wall.	☐	☐

2 Tick (✓) the correct answers. Only one answer is correct. (3 CP)

1 The climbing wall…
☐ closes in April until November.
☐ is closed from April until November.
☐ is only open in April and November.
☐ is closed from November until April.

2 Gary is surprised that…
☐ many teenagers prefer the salad bar over the Mexican restaurant.
☐ so many people eat at the Mexican restaurant.
☐ nobody notices that most of the food was frozen.
☐ Western people often eat tacos and tortillas.

3 Gary likes best about the Recreation Center…
☐ that you can see the Denver skyscrapers from the terrace.
☐ that the entrance fees are quite low.
☐ that it's eco-friendly.
☐ that it is really modern.

Schulaufgabe 7 — Workshop 4

→ students' book, pp. 109–113

3 Complete the statements. (7 CP)

Gary   We installed a _____ energy system on the roof to heat all the water, especially for the swimming pools, of course. Like that, we don't need energy from _____ _____ and we can help reduce carbon _____ in the Denver area.

Catherine That's excellent – you are reducing your carbon _____!

Gary   We also take care of the environment in our restaurants. Food isn't served in plastic containers, and we only sell water and other drinks in _____ bottles. Also, you will not find any plastic _____ in any of the restaurants! Or visitors can bring their own bottles, too. All the food _____ from the restaurants is used for making compost.

4 Answer the questions in complete sentences. (4 CP)

1 Explain what Gary means with 'sustainability is the key to protecting the environment.'
   _____
   _____

2 If you were a visitor at the Denver Paradise Recreation Center, which activity would you do? Give a reason for your answer.
   _____
   _____

2 Use of English: The Grand Canyon (On Track)

Mixed bag (30 CP)

Complete the sentences with the correct word or the correct form of the word in brackets. You may also need to add a negation, a modal or an auxiliary verb.

Chris and Kelly are talking about their 'Route 66' project.

Schulaufgabe 7 — Workshop 4
→ students' book, pp. 109–113

Chris Mrs Golding said our part of the 'Route 66 Project' is the state of Arizona, right?

Kelly That's right. Arizona and New Mexico, too.

Chris If our topic _____ (be) the state of California, we _____ (write) about Hollywood!

Kelly Yeah, but Arizona is an interesting state, too. Did you know that some parts of Arizona are still quite _____ (= not touched by humans)?
If we _____ (find) enough information,
we _____ (write) about the Grand Canyon.

Chris Cool! Let's do some internet research. We _____ (be) more effective if you _____ (sit down) right next to me.

Kelly OK. Where can we start? Let's type 'Grand Canyon' into the search engine.
Uuuh, so many results! If we _____ (want) to finish today,
we _____ (think) of a different search strategy.

Chris Good. Last week, Mrs Golding _____ (say) that there is a glass platform over the Grand Canyon. I can't remember its name!

Kelly If you _____ (pay) more attention, we _____ (waste) so much time already!

Chris I'm sorry. But wait, I think it was called 'The Grand Canyon Skywalk'.

Kelly Great. Let's see. Here. The text says that the Grand Canyon Skywalk is located on the Western _____ (= edge) of the Grand Canyon, on the Hualapai Indian Reservation, and it _____ (open) in 2007.
It is 4,000 feet above the ground. Tourists need a _____ (= document that allows you to do sth.) if they _____ (take) pictures.

Chris The Hualapai tribe actually saw some _____ (= positive aspects) in the Skywalk, didn't they?

Kelly Yes, they did. Many of the Hualapai people _____ (be) unemployed for ages before the opening of the Skywalk. Look at what one of them is saying today: 'If the Skywalk _____ (bring) so many tourists to the area, unemployment _____ (continue).'

Chris But some _____ (= people who care about the environment) said no one knew what _____ (= effect) the Skywalk would have on nature. It's important that you behave respectfully towards nature.

Kelly That's right. Let's see what else we can use.

Schulaufgabe 7 — Workshop 4

→ students' book, pp. 109–113

Chris The website also says that tourists _____ (enjoy) amazing views of the Grand Canyon if they _____ (book) a helicopter ride.

Kelly Well, I _____ (like) to watch the _____ (= when the sun goes down) over the Grand Canyon. I'm sure that's really romantic! What _____ (you / do) if you ever _____ (to go) to the Grand Canyon?

Chris I don't know. If I _____ (win) the lottery, I _____ (try) all the activities!

2 Use of English: The Grand Canyon (Fast Track)

Mixed bag (30 CP)

Complete the sentences with

.... → the correct word

_____ → the correct form of one the verbs from the box below. You may also need to add a negation, a modal or an auxiliary verb. You can use the verbs more than once.

> be ■ open ■ pay ■ say ■ sit down ■ take ■ think ■ want ■ waste ■ write

'The Grand Canyon'

Chris and Kelly are talking about their 'Route 66' project.

Chris Mrs Golding said our part of the 'Route 66 Project' is the state of Arizona, right?

Kelly That's right. Arizona and New Mexico, too.

Chris If our topic _____ the state of California, we _____ about Hollywood!

Kelly Yeah, but Arizona is an interesting state, too. Did you know that some parts of Arizona are still quite .... (= not touched by humans)? If we _____ enough information, we _____ about the Grand Canyon.

Schulaufgabe 7 — Workshop 4

→ students' book, pp. 109–113

Chris Cool! Let's do some internet research. We _____ more effective if you _____ right next to me.

Kelly OK. Where can we start? Let's type 'Grand Canyon' into the search engine. Uuuh, so many results! If we _____ to finish today, we _____ of a different search strategy.

Chris Good. Last week, Mrs Golding _____ that there is a glass platform over the Grand Canyon. I can't remember its name!

Kelly If you _____ more attention, we _____ so much time already!

Chris I'm sorry. But wait – I think it was called 'The Grand Canyon Skywalk'.

Kelly Great. Let's see. Here. The text says that the Grand Canyon Skywalk is located on the Western _____ (= *edge*) of the Grand Canyon, on the Hualapai Indian Reservation, and it _____ in 2007. It is 4,000 feet above the ground. Tourists need a _____ (= *document that allows you to do sth*) if they _____ pictures.

---

be ■ book ■ bring ■ continue ■ do ■ enjoy ■ go ■ like ■ try ■ win

---

Chris The Hualapai tribe actually saw some _____ (= *positive aspects*) in the Skywalk, didn't they?

Kelly Yes, they did. Many of the Hualapai people _____ unemployed for ages before the opening of the Skywalk. Look at what one of them is saying today: 'If the Skywalk _____ so many tourists to the area, unemployment _____.'

Chris But some _____ (= *people who care about the environment*) said no one knew what _____ (= *effect*) the Skywalk would have on nature. It's important that you behave respectfully towards nature.

Kelly That's right. Let's see what else we can use.

Chris The website also says that tourists _____ amazing views of the Grand Canyon if they _____ a helicopter ride.

Kelly Well, I _____ to watch the _____ (= *when the sun goes down*) over the Grand Canyon. I'm sure that's really romantic! What _____ if you ever _____ to the Grand Canyon?

Schulaufgabe 7 — Workshop 4
→ students' book, pp. 114–117

Chris   I don't know … If I _____ the lottery,

I _____ all the activities!

3 Mediation: Die Umwelt-AG (30 CP)

Demnächst wird Claire Watson, eine Schülerin aus Denver, Colorado, für einige Wochen deine Schule besuchen. Lies Claires Email und verfasse eine Antwort mit ca. 150 Wörtern. Nutze dazu die Informationen von dem Plakat, das du in der Pausenhalle deiner Schule entdeckt hast, und den Artikel von der Schulhomepage.

To: Claire Watson
From: _____
Subject: My trip to Germany!

Dear _____ ,

Thank you so much for helping me plan my stay in Germany. I'm really excited! I've never been on a different continent before! I'm also a bit nervous about the long-distance flight – all by myself …

But anyway, as you know, I am very interested in nature and the environment. Have I told you that I worked as a junior ranger in the national park? Which activities are there at your school?

See you soon!

Claire

Umwelt-AG!

„Erst wenn der letzte Baum gerodet, der letzte Fluss vergiftet, der letzte Fisch gefangen ist, werdet Ihr merken, dass man Geld nicht essen kann."

Ist das auch euer Wahlspruch? Dann seid ihr bei uns richtig!

Wer? Alle Schülerinnen und Schüler aus den Jahrgangsstufen 7 – 12
Wann? Montag in der 7. und 8. Stunde (13.10 – 14.40 Uhr); vierzehntägig
Wo? Raum A007, Neubau

Unsere Aktivitäten:

- Aktionen rund ums Recycling; Mülltrennung an der Schule
- nachhaltiges Handeln: Was kann ich zuhause tun?
- regelmäßige Treffen zum Mülleinsammeln auf dem Schulgelände und in der Stadt
- Ausbildung zum Energiemanager
- Organisation eines Energiespartags an der Schule (siehe auch Artikel auf unserer Homepage!, s. u.)

Wer teilnehmen möchte, kann einfach vorbeikommen. Oder schickt eure Ideen per Email an umwelttag@abc-gymnasium.de. Wir freuen uns auf euch!

Schulaufgabe 7

Workshop 4
→ students' book, pp. 114–117

| NEWS | TERMINE | KONTAKTE | BLOG | BILDER |

Bücherprämien für Energiesparen

Der Stromspartag am 12. Dezember war auch in diesem Schuljahr sehr erfolgreich. Mit Unterstützung der Energiemanager konnte wieder gezeigt werden, dass durch sinnvolles Ausschalten von Licht, Beamern und Computern der klimaschädliche CO_2-Ausstoß merklich verringert werden kann. Als Dankeschön für das Engagement spendete der Klimaschutzverein am Gymnasium neue Bücher im Wert von über 100 Euro für die Schülerlesebücherei. Die Bücherprämien wurden am Donnerstag, den 31.01. übergeben. Ein besonderer Dank geht an Frau Nieder für den Einkauf der Bücher und die hervorragende Betreuung unserer großen, vielfältigen Schülerbibliothek.

Wer auch zu Hause Möglichkeiten finden will, wie man Energie einsparen kann, kann sich immer freitags in der 2. Pause bei Herrn Schnell ein Energiemessgerät ausleihen und daheim den Stromverbrauch von Computer, Kühlschrank und Co. ermitteln.

# Schulaufgabe 8

Schulaufgabe 8 (88 CP)

1 Reading comprehension: Lilac's blog (24 CP)

Read Lilac's blog carefully and answer the questions on pages 64 and 65.

Sporty Lilac's football blog

February 9th

Hi guys! I'm sure you all watched the Super Bowl last Sunday! What a game! I loved the atmosphere – the entertainment, the fun, the concentration … I wish I would have been there!

Well, for my international followers, who might not be so familiar with American football, I'll explain a few things:

The Super Bowl, which usually takes place on the first Sunday in February each year, is the championship game of the National Football League (NFL) in which the champion of the National Football Conference (NFC) competes against the champion of the American Football Conference (AFC). The NFL's 17-week regular season runs from early September to late December. Each team plays 16 games. Altogether, there are 32 teams which play in the NFL. I'm a great Broncos fan. The team's full name is actually 'The Denver Broncos', but everyone I know just calls them the Broncos. Funny name, isn't it? A 'bronco' is a really strong and powerful horse. The term is Spanish, it comes from Mexico, and broncos are also used in rodeos. Anyway, it seems like a perfect name for the strong and wild players in the team! Whenever I watch them play in the stadium, they seem even wilder than on TV! I'm of course very proud that the Broncos of Mile High are currently the most successful team in the NFL. They play for the AFC West division, just like the Los Angeles Chargers, the Kansas City Chiefs, and the Oakland Raiders (= more funny names). So, why are the Broncos the greatest team? Because they won Super Bowl XXXII, Super Bowl XXXIII, and Super Bowl 50! And they are Denverites, like I am!

Take care and be sporty! See you all next week!

Lilac

February 16th

Hi guys! How's everybody doing? After my post last week, Daniel from Germany (he is one of my international followers) wondered why the competition is actually called 'Super Bowl' even if the trophy is not a bowl but an egg-shaped American football! It's normally silver.

So, why is the Super Bowl called Super Bowl?
Well, we have to go back in history really far. In 1923, a football championship, the Tournament of Roses, took place in the Rose Bowl Stadium in Pasadena. That's a city in California. The stadium's form looked like a large salad bowl, so that is why people called it the Rose Bowl Stadium.

© Westermann Gruppe

Because of the great popularity of the Tournament of Roses and its stadium, college football contests were created for Miami (the Orange Bowl), New Orleans (the Sugar Bowl), and El Paso (the Sun Bowl) in 1935, and for Dallas (the Cotton Bowl) in 1937. Now, we use the term 'bowl' for any major American football game – NFL, divisions, college level, and so on.

Daniel also wanted to know why there are letters on the trophy – like L, X, and I. That's strange, isn't it? Let me explain. Normally, they use Roman numbers to identify each game. For example, Super Bowl 1 took place on January 15, 1967, so the trophy had an 'I' (that's the Roman number 1) written on it. And so on and so on. There has been only one exception so far: Super Bowl 50 (in 2016) didn't get a Roman number. Another change to the tradition was that for the 50th Super Bowl the trophy was golden instead of silver. A lot nicer, if you ask me! But guess what happened in the following year. The Super Bowl number was 'LI'. So, can you guess what the 'L' means now? Please write back to me if you've got any more questions...

Take care and be sporty! See you all next week!

Lilac

February 22nd

Hi sporty girls and boys out there, how are you? Guess what – another fascinating question has reached me from Europe since my post two weeks ago: Deepak from the UK asked what I mean with 'Mile High'. I'm sorry if I haven't been precise. Of course I thought everybody knows what 'Mile High' is – it's the name of the Broncos' stadium here in Denver! The stadium's official name is 'Broncos Stadium at Mile High'. It's located exactly one mile above sea level. Of course we use it mainly for NFL games. On January 24, 2016, the Broncos defeated the New England Patriots in the AFC Championship Game 20–18 in front of a crowd of 77,100 people, and two weeks later, they won Super Bowl 50! The Carolina Panthers didn't have a chance. 24-10! But that game was in Santa Clara, California, unfortunately. Anyway, it seems as if the Southwest is really the center of American football!

So, let me tell you a bit more about Mile High. It also hosts other important events. Look, below I send you a link (it's not just about sports!).

In the meantime – remain sporty everybody!

Lilac

Schulaufgabe 8 — Workshop 4

→ students' book, pp. 120–127

| NEWS | DATES | CONTACT | BLOG | GALLERY |

Soccer

date	winning team	result	losing team	tournament	attendance[1]
July 26, 2014	Manchester United	3 – 2	A.S. Roma	International Champions Cup	54,116

Rugby

date	winner	score	opponent	league	attendance
June 23, 2018	England	36 – 18	New Zealand	Rugby League International Federation	19,320

Concerts

date	artist	attendance	revenue[2]	notes
August 11, 2001	Eagles	54,217	$4,837,465	first concert at the stadium
September 25, 2003	Bruce Springsteen	37,500	$2,442,072	
May 21, 2011	U2	77,900	$6,663,410	original date: June 12, 2010, but: Bono's emergency back surgery!
June 7, 2017	Metallica	57,027	$6,299,803	
August 2, 2017	Guns 'n' Roses	44,806	$3,846,068	
May 25, 2018	Taylor Swift	57,140	$7,926,366	first female solo artist at the stadium

---

[1] **attendance** all the people who come to see a match or concert.
[2] **revenue** all the money that is produced at a match or a concert, usually from ticket prices.

Schulaufgabe 8 — Workshop 4

→ students' book, pp. 120–127

1 Right or wrong? Tick the correct answers and correct the false statements. (8 CP)

		right	wrong
1	In the Super Bowl competition, the winner of the AFC and the winner of the NFL play against each other.	☐	☐
2	The people riding rodeos are called 'broncos'.	☐	☐
3	Lilac often watches the Broncos' games at the stadium in Denver.	☐	☐
4	The Denver Broncos have won the Super Bowl three times.	☐	☐
5	You can use the term 'Bowl' only for NFL games.	☐	☐

2 Tick (✓) the correct answers. Only one answer is correct. (4 CP)

1 The Super Bowl trophy …
☐ has always been silver.
☐ has been golden since the year 2016.
☐ is silver and golden at the same time.
☐ is normally silver, but not in the year 2016.

2 The 51st Super Bowl competition …
☐ took place in 2018.
☐ had the number 'LI'.
☐ had a clear winner: the Denver Broncos.
☐ didn't get a Roman number.

3 In January 2016,
☐ the New England Patriots won against the Denver Broncos.
☐ the Carolina Panthers won the Super Bowl.
☐ the Denver Broncos won against the New England Patriots.
☐ the Denver Broncos won the Super Bowl.

4 In Mile High Stadium,
☐ more than 90,500 people can watch the games.
☐ concerts and other sports events take place.
☐ there are more soccer games than American football games.
☐ the most expensive seat is one mile above the ground.

3 Complete the statements. (4 CP)

1 Lilac calls the American Southwest the 'center of American football' because

_____
_____
_____

© Westermann Gruppe

Schulaufgabe 8 — Workshop 4
→ students' book, pp. 120–127

2 Taylor Swift's concert at Mile High stadium on May 25, 2018 broke two records because

_____
_____
_____

4 **Answer the questions in complete sentences.** (4 CP)

1 At the end of her third blog, Lilac says: 'But that game was in Santa Clara, California, unfortunately'. Why does Lilac use 'unfortunately' here?

_____
_____
_____

2 Compare Lilac's blog with the tips Tariq gave Jeff about blogging. Which advice would you give Lilac?

_____
_____
_____
_____
_____

5 **Imagine you are one of Lilac's followers.** Think of two questions you could ask her. (4 CP)

_____
_____
_____
_____
_____

Schulaufgabe 8 — Workshop 4

→ students' book, pp. 120 – 127

2 Use of English: My favorite holiday (On Track)

Mixed tenses (24 CP)

Caleb and Lilac are talking about their favorite holidays. Complete the sentences with the correct form of the verbs in brackets. You may also need to add a modal or an auxiliary verb.

Caleb Lilac, you said in the interview that you like the fourth of July holiday best. Why?

Lilac It's mainly because I love the fireworks, and also because my aunt and uncle visit us every year on the fourth of July. If they _____ (*not come*) on the fourth of July, I _____ (*see*) them at all! But of course I also like the fourth of July because of its history. The United States of America _____ (*even / not exist*) if the thirteen colonies in New England _____ (*not declare*) independence on the fourth of July in the year 1776.

Caleb Yes, that's true. And we _____ (*belong to*) Great Britain if the Founding Fathers _____ (*not sign*) the Declaration of Independence!

Lilac Yeah, that's a funny thought, isn't it?

Caleb When I _____ (*watch*) the fireworks on the next fourth of July, I _____ (*surely / think*) of it!

Lilac Caleb, what's your favorite holiday? If I _____ (*remember*) correctly, it _____ (*be*) Thanksgiving, wasn't it?

Caleb Yes, that's right. I guess we'd all be very unhappy if we _____ (*not can / celebrate*) Thanksgiving. We love the food! Especially the roast turkey, of course.

Lilac I'm sure the turkey _____ (*be*) happier if you _____ (*eat*) less meat ...

Caleb Oh, Lilac! Are you a vegetarian now? Let me tell you something about the first Thanksgiving, you know, it _____ (*happen*) in 1621. The Pilgrims – that's the name of the first settlers – and the Native Americans _____ (*sit*) together, at one table. They _____ (*thank*) God that they were still alive! If the Native Americans _____ (*not show*) the Pilgrims how to grow

Schulaufgabe 8 — Workshop 4
→ students' book, pp. 120–127

corn and catch fish, they _____ (not survive) the first year in America.

Lilac   So, _____ (usually / you / help) with the food on Thanksgiving?

Caleb   Well, a little bit. If I _____ (have) time, I _____ (chop) the vegetables. Until I _____ (learn) how to cook a turkey properly, my Mum _____ (do) it.

Lilac   But just imagine: What would happen if you _____ (become) a vegetarian?

Caleb   No way!

2 Improve your style! (10 CP)

Read Ava's homework. It's an article for the *Rochester Daily News*. Her teacher has already underlined words and phrases that need to be changed to improve Ava's style. Write better words/phrases on the lines on the right. And mind the tenses, too.

Transatlantic friends at Rochester High School

We, some students at Rochester High School, have worked on a 'Transatlantic Friends Project'. Mrs Golding <u>wanted that we do</u> this project.   pe _____

In the project, we said <u>what is different between</u> our lives in the US and the lives of students our age in Europe.   co _____

At first, Mrs Golding <u>said it would be great</u> to <u>put our ideas into a good order</u>.   re _____
                                                                 se _____

So each student <u>gave</u> a little speech about a 'transatlantic topic' like food, school and sports.   de _____

We were all really careful not to <u>be rude to</u> anybody in the video conferences.   of _____

At the end of the project, everybody <u>talked about</u> their parts again.   re _____

We are all very grateful to Mrs Golding, who <u>watched</u> us all the time.   su _____

Schulaufgabe 8

Workshop 4
→ students' book, pp. 120–127

> We are sure that the 'Transatlantic Friends Project' touched us all in a positive way. We know so much about the European students now!
>
> Our next transatlantic project will be to do a survey on European holidays. For example we want to find out whether the Germans celebrate Thanksgiving, too.

af_____

co_____

2 Use of English: My favorite holiday (Fast Track)
Mixed tenses (24 CP)

Caleb and Lilac are talking about their favorite holidays. Fill in the gaps with the right form of one of the verbs below and the words given in brackets. You may also need to add a modal or an auxiliary verb. You can use the verbs more than once.

> be ■ belong ■ celebrate ■ come ■ declare ■ eat ■ exist ■
> see ■ sign ■ remember ■ watch

Caleb   Lilac, you said in the interview that you like the fourth of July holiday best. Why?

Lilac   It's mainly because I love the fireworks, and also because my aunt and uncle visit us every year on the fourth of July. If they _____ (not) on the fourth of July, I _____ (not) them at all!

But of course I also like the fourth of July because of its history. The United States of America _____ (even / not) if the thirteen colonies in New England _____ (not) independence on the fourth of July in the year 1776.

Caleb   Yes, that's true. And we _____ (still) Great Britain if the Founding Fathers _____ (not) the Declaration of Independence!

Lilac   Yeah, that's a funny thought, isn't it?

Caleb   When I _____ the fireworks on the next fourth of July, I _____ (surely) of it!

Schulaufgabe 8 — Workshop 4

→ students' book, pp. 120–127

Lilac Caleb, what's your favorite holiday? If I _____ correctly, it _____ Thanksgiving, wasn't it?

Caleb Yes, that's right. I guess we'd all be very unhappy if we _____ _____ (not can) Thanksgiving. We love the food! Especially the roast turkey, of course.

Lilac I'm sure the turkey _____ happier if you _____ less meat …

> become ■ chop ■ do ■ happen ■ have ■ help ■ learn ■ show ■ sit ■ survive ■ thank

Caleb Oh, Lilac! Are you a vegetarian now? Let me tell you something about the first Thanksgiving, you know, it _____ in 1621. The Pilgrims – that's the name of the first settlers – and the Native Americans _____ together, at one table. They _____ God that they were still alive! If the Native Americans _____ (not) the Pilgrims how to grow corn and catch fish, they _____ _____ (not) the first year in America.

Lilac So, _____ (usually / you) with the food on Thanksgiving?

Caleb Well, a little bit. If I _____ time, I _____ the vegetables. Until I _____ how to cook a turkey properly, my Mum _____ it.

Lilac But just imagine: What would happen if you _____ a vegetarian?

Caleb No way!

2 Improve your style! (10 CP)

Read Ava's homework. It's an article for the *Rochester Daily News*. Her teacher has already underlined words and phrases that need to be changed to improve Ava's style. Use the verbs in the box and write better words/phrases on the lines on the right.

> affect ■ compare ■ conduct ■ deliver ■ exploit ■ govern ■ host ■ influence ■ offend ■ persuade ■ recommend ■ reconstruct ■ review ■ sequence ■ supervise

Schulaufgabe 8 — Workshop 4

→ students' book, pp. 120–127

Transatlantic friends at Rochester High School

We, some students at Rochester High School, have worked on a 'Transatlantic Friends Project'. Mrs Golding <u>wanted us to do</u> this project.

In the project, we <u>said what is different between</u> our lives in the US and the lives of students our age in Europe.

At first, Mrs Golding <u>said it would be great to put our ideas into a good order.</u>

So each student <u>gave</u> a little speech about a 'transatlantic topic' like food, school and sports.

We were all really careful not to <u>be rude to</u> anybody in the video conferences.

At the end of the project, everybody <u>talked about</u> their parts again.

We are all very grateful to Mrs Golding, who <u>watched</u> us all the time.

We are sure that the 'Transatlantic Friends Project' <u>touched</u> us all in a positive way. We know so much about the European students now!

Our next transatlantic project will be to <u>do</u> a survey on European holidays. For example we want to find out whether the Germans celebrate Thanksgiving, too.

3 Writing: A gap year[1] in the American Southwest (30 CP)

Imagine you are spending a gap year in the American Southwest. At the moment, you are working as a Junior Ranger in the Grand Canyon National Park. Next week, you will return to high school in Santa Fe. Write an email to your best friend in Wales (!) and tell him / her about:
- your job at the National Park, the native population, ecotourism
- your school
- your plans for the rest of the year
- what your friend would / wouldn't like

Write about 150 words on an extra sheet.

---

[1] **gap year** When you take a one-year break, for example from school, university or your job.

Audioskripte

Track 1 (Schulaufgabe 1, Workshop 1)

Henry Hi everybody and welcome to the 45th edition of our podcast. You're listening to Hill End School FM, the best online radio station in the world! In our weekly podcast we give you a summary of the week's most important events, answer your questions and talk about topics which are important for our listeners, the students at Hill End School and millions of teenagers out there! I'm Henry.
Today we want to talk about a project called 'Hill End School goes green', which the school council started last week. Polly, the chair, talked to our reporter Aimee and explained the idea behind this project:

Aimee Polly, can you tell our listeners why the school council started the project 'Hill End School goes green'?

Polly A lot of students at our school are worried about nature. On the one hand, they see the dustbins which are filled with plastic bottles and so much litter. They watch the news reports about climate change and they understand that it's their future which is in danger. On the other hand, they feel helpless and don't know what they can do as a single person. But our school is a strong team, and together we can really change something and turn Hill End School into a green school, or at least a greener school. This is why we started our project 'Hill End School goes green', so that every student can help to protect our planet.

Aimee What were the students' reactions?

Polly Before we started the project, we did a survey in which we found out that 79 percent of the teenagers wish they could actively protect our nature and support the school council's project. Only 21 percent of the people who answered our questions are not motivated enough. So, we knew it wouldn't be a problem to find enough members. Up to now, 189 students have signed up for the project on our website and we can hardly read all the ideas they have sent us.

Henry That sounds great! But what exactly are your ideas? Our reporter Aimee did a second interview for Hill End School FM and tried to find out how YOU would like to turn Hill End School into a green school.

Aimee Hi! What's your name?

Simon Hi, my name is Simon and I'm 14.

Aimee What's your opinion on the school council's project?

Simon Of course I want to protect our nature! I've already signed up for the project because I've got so many ideas. For example, I think that we should use less paper at our school, so we could protect our trees and our forests. The teachers should hand out less photocopies ... Maybe they could send us emails with the worksheets. Actually, I hope that one day every student has got a laptop and doesn't have real books anymore. I know it's expensive, but in the long run it's certainly much cheaper than all the paper which is no longer necessary.

Aimee Ok, and what's your name?

Lily Hi, my name is Lily and I'm 12.

Aimee Are you going to join 'Hill End School goes green'?

Lily No, I'm not. I think that you needn't be in a team to actively protect the environment. I live on a farm near Durham and my parents have taught me how to respect nature.

Aimee Can you give us some examples?

Lily Yes, of course. Since we have got lots of different vegetables and fruit, we don't buy products which have travelled a long distance by plane. I don't want to eat tomatoes in February, I can have cabbage instead.

Aimee I understand what you mean, but unfortunately most of us don't live on a farm ...

Lily Yes, I know, but most of us could buy local products on a farm instead of exotic products in a supermarket. And if we buy fewer products in a supermarket, we have less plastic.

Aimee I agree. Maybe we could sell some of your products in our school shop... Oh and there's a student who is already wearing a 'Hill End School goes green' button. What's your name?

Lucas Hi, my name is Lucas and I'm 13.

Aimee I guess you've already signed up for the new project?

Lucas I don't need to, I'm a member of the school council and one of the students who have organized the project.

Aimee Oh, I see. So what exactly would you like to change at Hill End School?

Lucas I think we should have more school busses so that parents don't need to take their children to school by car. And we need to build new bike

	sheds for those students who come to school by bike, which is the healthiest and best solution for our environment.
Henry	Well, I see that the school council has created a project which will be a success and which most of you are going to support actively. I'm sure that we will talk about it again very soon. Take care and join us again next week for the 46th edition of our podcast! I'm Henry for Hill End School FM.

Track 2 (Schulaufgabe 4, Workshop 2)

Vivian	Hello Mrs O'Brian. How are you?
Mrs O'Brian	Hello Vivian! Good to see you! I'm fine. Shauna hasn't finished her homework yet, I'm sorry, but she'll be with us in a few minutes. Maybe you can help me while you are waiting for her?
Vivian	What are you doing, Mrs O'Brian? Why are you decorating your living room in green?
Mrs O'Brian	It's 17 March!
Vivian	Is it your birthday today?
Mrs O'Brian	No, it isn't. It's St Patrick's Day, Vivian, don't you remember?
Vivian	Oh, yes, of course I do! Has Shauna told you about our history project? We've learned a lot about American history and the countries the immigrants came from. I think that I finally understand why you celebrate St Patrick's Day …
Mrs O'Brian	Yes, St Patrick's Day is an Irish tradition and our family is of Irish origin.
Vivian	Did your ancestors come to America on the Mayflower?
Mrs O'Brian	No, they didn't. They were not among the first settlers, they immigrated much later. My ancestor Conor O'Brian left Ireland in the 19th century. He was born in 1827 and he grew up in the south of Ireland in a very big family, he actually had four brothers and five sisters. His parents had a small farm, some fields where they could plant crops, and just enough cattle to feed the family. Basically he had a happy childhood.
Vivian	But why did he leave his home country then?
Mrs O'Brian	From 1845 to 1849, there was a terrible catastrophe which destroyed most of the potatoes in Ireland. It led to what people called 'The Great Famine', which means that most of the Irish people were very hungry because there was not enough food. Many people were starving. This is why Conor left Ireland in 1847. He wanted to go to the USA to look for better living conditions, as thousands of people had done before him.
Vivian	Oh, I see … It's really hard to imagine such a situation today.
Mrs O'Brian	Yes, it is. But life was different back then. People could not just go to a supermarket and buy products from foreign countries which had not been affected by this catastrophe. These supermarkets simply did not exist and the trade system was limited to very few products. And even if there had been the possibility to buy food, Conor's family wouldn't have had enough money. As a consequence, his family was starving, too. In his diary we can read that he had to go to bed with an empty stomach and if he was lucky, there was a little slice of bread for breakfast. He was the eldest son of the family, so his father decided to send him to the USA where he should start a new life.
Vivian	How did he travel?
Mrs O'Brian	First he had to take the train to get to the port where he boarded a ship. We know quite a lot about the journey from his diary. They left Ireland when the sun was shining and the sea was calm, so the first part of the voyage seemed to be easy. All the people were looking forward to their new life in the New World. Unfortunately, the situation changed drastically after the first three days. Conor described a terrible storm which turned the sea into a rough place and made the ship shake heavily while it was fighting against the dangerous waves. Conor must have been deeply scared and seasick all the time. And he must have been terribly relieved when he finally reached the USA after 24 days.
Vivian	But why did he travel alone?
Mrs O'Brian	The family could not afford tickets for the other children. They hoped that Conor would make a lot of money in the New World and send it to Ireland, and this is exactly what he did. Four of his brothers and sisters followed him five years later when conditions were better.
Vivian	How did your family's story continue?
Mrs O'Brian	Conor worked as a mechanic and he was very successful. When he was 32 years old, he got married and had four children with his wife Andrea, whose family was of German origin. So my great-great-grandfather James grew up in a family which kept alive Irish and German traditions, and he learned to speak both languages.
Vivian	Oh, now I know why Shauna is so good at German! She has never told me before!
Mrs O'Brian	Well, actually we don't speak German at home anymore, but there are some traditions which we don't want to lose, and Shauna loves

	German food, especially the cakes which are so delicious!
Vivian	And these Irish and German traditions have influenced your family's history until today?
Mrs O'Brian	Yes, indeed. We think that these traditions are very important and also, it's important to know your family's origins and to keep alive typical traditions. Look, there's Shauna.
Shauna	Hi, Vivian!
Mrs O'Brian	And this must be Neil and Mary, my cousins. Let's say hello to them and start our very special St Patrick's Day!

Track 3 (Schulaufgabe 6, Workshop 3)

David	So, Dad, when are we going to eat at the pub? You know, Mum promised! Look, I've found this website called 'Riverside pubs'. They list all the pubs along the canal in the Llangollen area. In Ellesmere alone, there are seven pubs located directly at the canal.
Mr Sinclair	OK, David, let's see. Oh, that's fantastic! The website even tells us the exact name of the nearest lock, so that we know where to moor!
David	Look, Dad, there's a pub called 'The Red Lion'. It's got an interesting name, hasn't it?
Mr Sinclair	Yes, that's right. A few weeks ago, I read in the newspaper that 'Red Lion' was the most common pub name in the UK. Can you believe it, there are 632 pubs altogether with that particular name!
David	That's amazing! So there must be one in every town and village in Wales, too! Do you know anything about the history of this name?
Mr Sinclair	Of course I do! The origin of the Red Lion pub name dates back hundreds of years. Some historians think it derives from the heraldic coat of arms of a knight called John of Gaunt. He used a red lion as a symbol of his power. John of Gaunt died in 1399.
David	Wow! How interesting! I am really impressed, Dad!
Mr Sinclair	As we're going to have dinner at the 'Red Lion' – have you read anything about the menu yet?
David	Sure! Look, they offer some pub classics like farm pork sausages with garden peas, gravy, black pudding and mashed potatoes for just £ 8.95!
Mr Sinclair	Ok, sounds great. But are they serving anything vegetarian, too? You know, Mum will want something without meat.
David	I know, just wait a minute; I'll check again … Here, I have found a pasta dish with mushrooms, ham and garlic bread. It's only £8.95 as well.
Mr Sinclair	But David, ham is not exactly vegetarian …
David	Oh, yes, that's true. But you needn't be so bossy! … Anyway, she can always order a salad – there are plenty of salad dishes on the menu, too! I'm sure she's going to have the one with the roast vegetables. And just look at the list of desserts! You can't complain about that! Desserts are mainly vegetarian, aren't they, Dad?
Mr Sinclair	Oh David … But while you're at it, could you also check whether dogs are allowed in the pub? It won't be fun for Coco to stay on the boat alone!
David	Alright, let me see … I can't find any information on this. You know what? I am going to call the pub.
Mr Sinclair	That's a great idea, David. Then you can also make a reservation for 7 p.m. tomorrow, for six people and one cheeky dog.
David	Sure, I will! Thank you, Dad! I'll choose a burger, definitely. With extra chips and a double dessert, of course …
Mr Sinclair	Oh David, you're going to be so sick …

Track 4 (Schulaufgabe 7, Workshop 4)

Catherine	Welcome, listeners, to 'Denver Radio Rocky Mountains'. My name is Catherine and I'm your host today. In our show, we're presenting a variety of things to do in Denver every week – for people from Denver, from other parts of the US and from all around the world. You will be surprised how much this city has to offer for everybody! If you get a chance to visit any time of the year, I promise you'll never forget it! Let's start with some facts about Denver. Denver is the capital of the state of Colorado and it's located just on the eastern side of the Rocky Mountains. Denver got its name from James W. Denver, a former governor, and the city is nicknamed the 'mile high city' because its official height is exactly one mile above sea level. With a population of around 700,000 inhabitants, Denver is the 19th most populous US city. At the same time, Denver is the second largest city in the West after Phoenix, Arizona. So, what has Denver got to offer if you want to spend a great day with the family? Why not visit

	the Denver Paradise Recreation Center? It's Denver's newest recreation center – it only opened last year! Now, let's welcome Gary Miles to the show! He's the general manager of the Denver Paradise Recreation Centre! Hi, Gary, how're you doing?
Gary	Hi, Catherine, great! Thanks for having me on your show today.
Catherine	Gary, our leisure tip for our listeners today is the Denver Paradise Recreation Center. What can your guests expect there?
Gary	You can choose between a large, a small and a children's swimming area, or – if you are up for more action – there are also two diving boards and a water slide. You can also exercise at the gymnasium, which offers a basketball and a volleyball field. If you are even more adventurous, you could also try the slackline or the outdoor climbing wall. But please note that the climbing wall is closed between November and April every year.
Catherine	Fantastic! And what can people do if they get hungry after all these activities?
Gary	Oh, that's not a problem at all! If you are hungry, you can visit one of the three restaurants and snack bars at the Denver Paradise Recreation Center at any time. One offers Mexican food, like tacos or tortillas with various fillings, one serves mainly American food, and the third one is a salad counter with only fresh food – nothing comes from a freezer! All of them are popular, but the salad bar has recently developed into something like a favorite – even among teenagers, would you believe that?
Catherine	Gary, tell us, what's the best aspect about the Denver Paradise Recreation Center?
Gary	Well, that's difficult to answer … You know, I think it's a fantastic facility. I like everything about it! The pools, the view from the terrace when the sun sets behind the skyscrapers, its easy accessibility … Of course I have to admit that the entrance fees are not exactly cheap … But probably the thing I am proudest of is that Denver Paradise Recreation Center is extremely eco-friendly.
Catherine	Sounds great! Please tell us more about it!
Gary	We installed a solar energy system on the roof to heat all the water, especially for the swimming pools, so that we don't need energy from fossil fuels. This means we can reduce carbon emissions in the Denver area.
Catherine	That's excellent – so you reduce your carbon footprint!
Gary	We also take care of the environment in our restaurants. Food isn't served in plastic containers, and we only sell water and other drinks in reusable bottles. Also, you will not find any plastic cutlery in any of the restaurants! Or visitors can bring their own bottles, too. And the food waste from the restaurants is used for making compost.
Catherine	That's a really useful idea!
Gary	Sure, sustainability is the key to protecting the environment.
Catherine	Thank you so much, Gary, for joining us on the show today!
Gary	It was my pleasure!
Catherine	So guys, it is no surprise that Denver received the title 'best place to live in the US' by the US News & World Report last year. Pack your suitcases, step onto a plane or into your car, and meet Denver! It'll be worth it! For more information, give us a call on 1800 …

Answer key

Schulaufgabe 1

1 Listening comprehension (p. 9)

1 (8 CP; 1 CP pro richtige Antwort)

	Henry	Aimee	Polly	Simon	Lily	Lucas	none of them
a … likes the new project.	☐	☐	☒	☒	☐	☒	☐
b … is not going to take part in the new project.	☐	☐	☐	☐	☒	☐	☐
c … presents the podcast.	☒	☐	☐	☐	☐	☐	☐
d … has interviewed students at Hill End School.	☐	☒	☐	☐	☐	☐	☐
e … wants to collect money for the project.	☐	☐	☐	☐	☐	☐	☒
f … is the most important member of the school council.	☐	☐	☒	☐	☐	☐	☐

2 (3 CP)
The correct diagram is B (79 %).

3 (2 CP; 1 CP pro richtige Lücke)
Up to now, **189** students want to take part in the project. Those who want to join 'Hill End School goes green' can sign up on the school council's **website**.

4 (7 CP; 1 CP pro richtige Antwort)

Simon
☐ wants to have less books because his schoolbag is too heavy.
☒ wants to get less printed worksheets.
☐ wants to ban plastic bottles at his school.
☒ thinks that digital books help to protect our nature.
☐ has signed up via email.
☒ thinks that laptops will be less expensive than books if they are used for several years.

Lily
☐ likes exotic vegetables.
☐ is a vegetarian.
☒ prefers regional products.
☒ thinks that buying vegetables on a farm helps reduce plastic waste.
☐ has got a button with the project's slogan.

Lucas
☒ has got a button with the project's slogan.
☐ thinks that busses are bad for the environment.
☐ usually goes to school by bike.
☐ wants the students to walk to school.
☒ doesn't like parents who take their children to school by car.

2 Use of English (On / Fast Track, pp. 10–13)

30 CP (1 CP pro richtige Lücke)
At our last meeting, the members of the school council **talked** about their activities, plans and ideas. Life at our school **has already improved** a lot, but some problems **haven't been solved yet**. Let's start with the **improvements**: The principal **has already banned unhealthy** food and **plastic** bottles from our canteen and the school **has bought** more computers for the library. However, the principal **hasn't reacted** to our last wish list yet, which means that the text for the school's website about our charity event **hasn't been written** so far and that the students who **have never travelled** to Germany before still **don't know** if they can take part in this year's exchange programme.
At the moment the school council **is planning** to start a new project called 'Helping Hands at Hill End School', **which** could create many opportunities to take **responsibility**. Students from our school can help old people, for example they can do the shopping or take their dogs for a walk. Last week we **met** the principal who **said**: 'I'm sure that this project **will turn out** to be a big **success** very soon and that the people will be very **grateful** in the future.'
As you know Durham **chose** a new **mayor** in the **election** last Sunday and we**'ve already analysed** the promises **he has made so far** during his **campaign**. We are going to meet him next Thursday, but instead of chatting, we are going to **challenge** him in an interview because we want to learn more about his **opinion** on topics which are important for the younger generation. Let's see if he's still the **confident** person he **has been so far**.
If there are any questions you would like us to ask him, send us an email (schoolcouncil@hillendschool.co.uk).

3 Mediation (pp. 13–15)

Max. 30 CP

Sophie I really like your school, but the building is huge! And there are posters everywhere … I guess that there are lots of great events, but I don't understand most of the information. What about this poster, what is it about?
You It's about the school council meeting. All students are invited.
Sophie When and where does this meeting take place?
You The meeting will take place on Tuesday, October 5th, from 13.30 to 14.40 in the gym.

Sophie	What are the members of the school council going to do or talk about?
You	There are three things on the agenda. First, they are going to elect the new student representatives. Then they are going to plan the school council's Christmas concert. In the end, they will present and give an award to the best school logo. This logo will also be on the new school council collection which they are going to present.
Sophie	Sounds interesting. Can we go there, too?
You	**1 Yes, we can, because all students are invited.**
	2 Yes, we can, but we have to ask our teachers and the head teacher for permission because we have history and ICT at that time.
Sophie	Oh, what a pity! I'm sure that many students who can't go there have good ideas, too. But their ideas won't be heard.
You	**Students who have a good idea or suggestion can send their suggestions in an email before the meeting.**
Sophie	Alright, so let's continue our tour of the school building. Maybe we'll find some good ideas…

Schulaufgabe 2

1 Writing (p. 16)

Max. 30 CP

Beispiele:

Dear Mr …
- my name is … and I'm an exchange student from …
- I'm writing to you because I am quite unhappy about some things at your school.
- I've noticed that the canteen offers a lot of unhealthy food, like burgers and French fries …
- I think it is important to eat healthily, so I suggest that the canteen should offer different food as well, for example more vegetables.
- The canteen sells mainly sweets but not much fruit …
- Also, a lot of drinks in the canteen are sold in plastic bottles
- This causes too much litter. The school should recycle more waste …
- Students should use glasses instead of plastic bottles …

2 Use of English (On / Fast Track, pp. 17–20)

30 CP; 2 CP pro Satz

Aimee	Why doesn't dad look at his mobile phone and read his messages? **I've already sent him four text messages!**
Mrs Gordon	Oh look, there he is … Finally!
Aimee	**Dad, where have you been?**
Mr Gordon	**I've just visited the museum.** What a wonderful exhibition! **Have you seen the great paintings yet?**
Aimee:	Yes, I have.
Mrs Gordon	**Where did you start the tour this morning?**
Mr Gordon	**First, I went to the second floor.** Then I had lunch at the cafeteria.
Mrs Gordon	Without us? Why?
Mr Gordon	Sorry, dear. You seem to be quite upset. **How long have you been waiting for me?**
Aimee	**We've been sitting here since 1 o'clock.**
Mrs Gordon	**Why didn't you read my text messages?**
Mr Gordon	I'm sorry **but I've forgotten my mobile phone in the car.** **What have you been doing until now?**
Aimee	**I've been listening to the audio guide for half an hour.** **Mum has been reading her book since half past one.**
Mr Gordon	Which book?
Aimee	The book **which she bought in the shop when we left the museum without you.**
Mr Gordon	I'm really sorry. Do you want to come back to the second floor with me? The paintings there are fascinating!
Aimee	Oh no, Dad! I want to go home!!!

3 Reading comprehension (pp. 21–23)

1 (4 CP; 1 CP pro richtige Antwort)

1
Yes, he can make this statue because **Deepak found plastic bottles**.

2
No, he can't make this because **Deepak didn't find plants**.

3
Yes, he can make this car because **Deepak found carton packaging**.

4
No, he can't make this chair and table **because he didn't find wood**.

2 (6 CP; 1 CP pro richtige Antwort)

Who thinks that …	Deepak	Caroline	Jeremy	Sharon	Martin	Not in the text
… there should be less pollution in his or her home town.	☒	☐	☐	☐	☐	☐

Answer key

… it's a good idea to use old things again in a different way.	☒	☒	☐	☒	☒	☐
… people who leave plastic bags in a park should be reported to the police.	☐	☐	☐	☐	☐	☒

3 (5 CP; 1 CP pro richtige Antwort)

1
☐ turn Hill End School into a greener school.
☐ reduce the number of plastic bottles at his school.
☒ protect our nature.
☒ actively change situations which he doesn't like.

2
☒ has been thrown out of a car.
☐ you could eat.
☒ was wet.

☐ was very dangerous.
☐ was very heavy.
☒ was difficult to see.

4 (5 CP; 1 CP pro richtige Antwort)

	right	wrong	not in the text
1 'Upcycling' means that you simply repair something.	☐	☒	☐
2 Caroline has never used old clothes for upcycling.	☐	☐	☒
3 Caroline wants to use plastic bottles in her garden.	☐	☒	☐
4 Jeremy wants people to buy products which don't need a lot of plastic.	☒	☐	☐
5 Sharon likes to help poor people with her creative ideas	☒	☐	☐

Schulaufgabe 3

1 Reading comprehension (pp. 24–26)

1 (6 CP, 1 CP pro richtige Überschrift)
A: Thanksgiving: an all-American party for the whole family
B: History
C: Food
D: Football
E: Turkey Pardon
F: Anti-Thanksgiving campaigns

2 (7 CP; 1 CP je richtige Antwort)

	right	wrong	not in the text
1 The tradition of Thanksgiving began in the 16th century. *It began in the 17th century (1621).*	☐	☒	☐
2 It started with a Native American who helped people from England who were very hungry.	☒	☐	☐
3 He told the new settlers not to kill any animals. *He taught them how to hunt and how to grow crops.*	☐	☒	☐
4 He helped them even though he didn't understand their language.	☐	☐	☒
5 The first ceremony was organised by the Native Americans to welcome the new settlers. *It was organized by the settlers to thank the Lord. It was a big party for the Native Americans.*	☐	☒	☐
6 The tradition of Thanksgiving reminds us of the good relationship between Native Americans and the early English settlers.	☒	☐	☐
7 Thanks to Theodore Roosevelt, most Americans don't have to go to work or to school on Thanksgiving. *Abraham Lincoln made Thanksgiving a national holiday in 1861.*	☐	☒	☐

3 (1 CP)
24 November.

4 (5 CP; 1 CP pro richtige Antwort)

1
☐ for Native Americans.
☐ for people who prefer sweet dishes.
☒ for people who want to eat a lot of meat.
☐ for children.
☐ for people who are allergic to meat.
☒ for people who don't want to eat meat.

2
☒ big sport events are more important on Thanksgiving than going to church.
☐ it's important to thank God and to go to church on Thanksgiving.
☐ people need to do sports after Thanksgiving.
☐ it's fun to play American football with your friends on Thanksgiving.

Answer key

3
- ☐ didn't want to have a turkey.
- ☐ decided that no turkeys should be killed for Thanksgiving.
- ☐ received two turkeys as a gift.
- ☒ received three turkeys as a gift.
- ☒ decided that one of his turkeys shouldn't be killed.
- ☐ made Thanksgiving a national holiday.

5 (6 CP, max. 3 CP pro Frage)

1
Every year the American President, who usually gets several turkeys as a present, decides that one of them should not be killed. This decision is a symbol both of his power and of his ability to forgive.

2
Many Native Americans died from diseases which the white settlers had brought to America. Also, many of them were killed by white settlers. Even today, many suffer from poverty.

2 Use of English (On / Fast Track, pp. 27/28)

30 CP; 1 CP pro richtige Lücke
Most of the children of our **generation** in the USA know the famous story about their **ancestors** and their **origin**, which they can find in almost every history **textbook**.
In the past, many **brave** people went on a **voyage** to the New World. Among them there were **explorers** who wanted to discover the New World, **European settlers** who wanted to build new **colonies**, **servants** who wanted to have a better life in freedom and **religious** people who left England because of their **beliefs**. All of them wanted to live **happily** in **peace** without any wars and without **hunger**.
The **rough** journey by ship was usually very **long** and **dangerous**. At the beginning, all the people on the **deck** of the ship were **strangers** who had **nervously** left their families, but they **certainly** got to know each other very **quickly**. When they **successfully** arrived in the New World, the **survivors** of the journey **anxiously** left the ship. During the following years they usually got on quite **well**, they worked very **hard** and **slowly** improved their new life.

3 Writing (p. 29)

Max. 30 CP
Individuelle Antworten

Schulaufgabe 4

1 Listening comprehension (pp. 30/31)

1 (3 CP; 1 CP pro Lücke)
March 17, St. Patrick' Day

2 (1 CP)
Ireland / south of Ireland

3 (4 CP; 1 CP pro richtiges Jahr)

year	event
1827	Conor was born.
1845 – 1849	'Great Famine'
1847	Conor emigrated to the USA.

4 (2 CP; 1 CP pro richtige Antwort)
Conor's life was very difficult before he went to the USA because …
- ☐ the supermarket was too far away.
- ☒ there was not enough food.
- ☐ all the animals on his parents' farm had died.
- ☒ his family was very poor.
- ☐ his family had to sell the fields.
- ☐ he didn't find a job.

5 (2 CP; 1 CP pro richtige Antwort)
Zug, Schiff

6 (4 CP; 1 CP pro richtige Antwort)

	right	wrong
1 Conor travelled without any of the other members of his family.	☒	☐
2 The journey was very dangerous right from the start.	☐	☒
3 Mrs O'Brian knows a lot about his journey from the letters he sent to his family.	☐	☒
4 The journey took 34 days.	☐	☒

7 (4 CP; 1 CP pro richtige Lücke)
Conor started a new life in the USA, where he worked as a **mechanic**. When he was **32** years old, he started a family with his wife Andrea, who was of **German** origin. Shauna's family loves some of her traditions, too, especially the delicious **cakes / food**.

2 Use of English (On / Fast Track, pp. 32 – 34)

30 CP; 1 CP pro richtige Antwort
James is one of the best football players at Hill End School. He started to play **earlier than** his friends. He can kick the ball **harder than** the other boys in his team and he can run **the fastest**. In an **average** match he usually scores three goals.

Yesterday, however, he played **worse than** before. He was **obviously** in a bad **mood** because his coach wanted him to play **differently**. He doesn't like any kind of **criticism** and always

Answer key

wants to be perfect. In the middle of the match he **committed** a foul and spoke rather **unkindly** to the **referee** on the **pitch**. When the other team scored a **penalty**, he complained **immediately**. After the match he **disappeared** very **quickly** and I met him in the changing room where nobody wanted to talk to him or **disturb** him. He was very thirsty, but he didn't have a bottle, so I gave him **mine**. Of course he didn't thank me. In the evening, his sister tried to cheer him up and **switched** on the radio. Unfortunately, the song that was played sounded very **sad**. So he still felt very **bad** and looked **unhappy**. He even didn't like his sandwich, which **certainly** tasted **delicious**, so his sister gave him **hers**. But he was still hungry and before his parents could eat their sandwiches, he even ate **theirs**, too. At 10 o'clock he **finally** went to bed. His sister didn't want to wake him up again, so she walked past his door very **slowly** and closed the door to her room as **carefully** as she could. You see, James actually can be quite complicated.

3 Mediation (pp. 35–37)

Max. 30 CP

Beispiellösung:

Alessandro	Can you tell us more about the challenges of the next competition?
You	**For the next competition, we will have to show that we speak English very well. We will also have to learn and present a short text.**
Julie	What's important for Matthias?
You	**For Matthias, it is important that actors are good at English. Also, all participants must work as a team.**
Malte	I didn't remember my lines in the last rehearsal and I'm sure that I won't succeed. Is there any alternative for me if I don't want to be an actor?
You	**Yes, there is. You can also work behind the stage and be part of the crew, for example help with the costumes or the sound. Or you could also be a stage designer and decide how the stage is going to look …**
Pierre	So you can go on even if you don't know the script?!
You	**No, everybody has to know the script because the crew has to make sure that they are prepared for a new scene and choose the right sounds / music / light …**
Pierre	But these jobs are much less important, I'm sure he thinks so, too!
You	**No, he thinks that these jobs are also important. For example the sound designers have to make sure that the audience can hear the actors. Otherwise the audience will be disappointed. Without the team, the actors won't be successful …**

Anyway, I'm sure we're on the right track since we're a good English-speaking team with different abilities. Let's keep our fingers crossed for the challenge…

Schulaufgabe 5

1 Reading (p. 38–40)

1 (8 CP; 1 CP pro richtige Antwort, 1 CP pro korrigierte falsche Antwort)

	right	wrong
1 The Afanc is a scary ghost. *The Afanc is a sea monster.*	☐	☒
2 The actions of the Afanc were a big problem for the farmers of Conwy valley.	☒	☐
3 When the farmers tried to kill the Afanc, he came out and ate them alive. *He ate people who swan in his lake.*	☐	☒
4 The Afanc is very similar to Nessie, the Scottish monster.	☒	☐
5 The Afanc was very brutal and killed people for no reason. *He killed them when they annoyed him.*	☐	☒

2 (4 CP; 1 CP pro richtige Antwort)

1 The people of the valley decided to
☐ buy more arrows and spears from a better blacksmith.
☐ move the Afanc into a cave.
☐ throw a beautiful girl into the water to feed him.
☒ move the Afanc onto the other side of Mount Snowdon.

2 When the Afanc didn't come out of the lake, the people
☐ didn't know what to do.
☐ invited Hu Gardan to help them.
☒ needed a beautiful girl who could help them.
☐ were frustrated and gave up.

3 The Afanc
☐ heard the beautiful girl sing and jumped out of the lake.
☐ heard the iron chains and was afraid.
☒ heard the girl sing and slowly came out of the lake.
☐ attacked the girl because he didn't like her singing.

4 It was quite difficult
☒ for the oxen to pull the Afanc out of the water.
☐ for the girl to remember her song.
☐ for the blacksmith to concentrate.
☐ for the oxen to swim.

3 (4 CP; 1 CP pro richtige Antwort)

1 … became very angry and went back into the water.
2 … one of the oxen lost an eye because it was so hard to pull the Afanc up a mountain. The oxen's tears filled the pool with its tears.

Answer key

4 (4 CP; 2 CP pro richtige Antwort)
1 The people believed that they were safe in the end because around the lake there were many stones that would keep the Afanc inside it / so that he couldn't break out.
2 Bex is afraid of caves because one legend about the Afanc says that he is still living inside a Welsh cave.

2 Use of English (On Track / Fast Track, pp. 41–43)

30 CP (1 CP pro richtige Lücke)

David	So, Dad, what **are we going to do** in Llangollen?
Mr Sinclair	Well, there are many **nearby** attractions we can visit. I am very interested in the Llangollen Motor Museum. Its website says that we can see more than sixty vehicles, and some of them are still drivable. Most of the cars and motorcycles are really **old-fashioned**, too – from my **childhood**! I remember how I **had** a motorcycle accident when I was a young man.
David	**Did you hurt yourself?**
Mr. Sinclair	Yes, unfortunately, I **broke** my left leg. I **didn't drive** very **gently**.
David	Oh, you**'ve / have never told** me!
Mr Sinclair	I know, I **was ashamed** of **myself**.
David	That's nothing to be ashamed of, Dad.
Mr Sinclair	Well, it's a long time ago. Let's not worry – *(leer)* about the past. Let's talk about the future! Maybe **we are going to travel** on the Llangollen Railway. The journey is a relaxing ten miles and goes through the stunning Dee Valley to the lovely town of Corwen in North Wales. I **have always wanted** to travel on a **peaceful** historic train, which transported **goods / things** such as food and coal in the past. Ok, but I'm sure you **will be bored** after only a few minutes.
David	That's not true! I'**ll / will just need** some snacks.
Mr Sinclair	All right, let's concentrate – *(leer)* on our plans. The LLangollen Railway website also says that visitors **will enjoy** stunning views over the Dee valley.
David	But that **sounds totally** boring!
Mr Sinclair	Why? I **thought** you were interested in trains!
David	But Dad! I**'m not** five years anymore! You**'ve just mentioned** the River Dee: What about wild water rafting?
Mr Sinclair	That's actually not a bad idea. Let me see – the website says that the staff **will give** us all the equipment we need.
David	And we can help **each other** with the wetsuits!
Mr Sinclair	OK then, the afternoon trip **starts** at 1.30 pm. It'll be fun!

3 Writing (p. 44)

Max. 30 CP

Individuelle Lösungen in Form einer E-Mail mit folgenden Aspekten:

- Formalia einer E-Mail (Kopf, Anrede, Schlussformen)
- Informationen zu allen fünf Aspekten (Wie kommt man dort hin? Wo wird übernachtet? Wie waren das Wetter, die Leute, das Essen etc.? Nenne zwei Aktivitäten, die ihr in der ersten Woche unternommen habt; Berichte von euren Plänen für die zweite Woche)

Schulaufgabe 6

1 Listening comprehension (pp. 45/46)

1 (8 CP; 1 CP pro richtige Antwort; 1 CP pro korrigierte falsche Antwort)

	right	wrong
1 David found a website about pubs along the canal, with information on the nearest lock and the mooring prices.	☐	☒
The mooring prices are not mentioned.		
2 Mr Sinclair likes the website.	☒	☐
3 Mr Sinclair read an article on pub names on the Internet.	☐	☒
He read an article in the newspaper.		
4 In the UK there are over 700 pubs with the name 'The Red Lion'.	☐	☒
There are 632 pubs with this name.		
5 David believes that many pubs in Wales are called 'The Red Lion'.	☒	☐

2 (3 CP; 1 CP pro richtige Antwort)
1c, 2b, 3d

3 (3 CP; 1 CP pro richtige Antwort)
true, bossy, complain

4 (4 CP; 2 CP pro richtige Antwort)
1 David is going to call the pub to find out whether they are allowed to bring their dog, Coco, into the pub.
2 Mr Sinclair is worried that David is going to be sick when he eats everything he says he's going to eat at the 'Red Lion': a burger with extra chips and dessert.

2 Use of English (On / Fast Track; pp. 46–52)

1 (24 CP; 1 CP pro richtige Lücke)

Mrs Sinclair	So, Bex, have you got much homework?
Bex	It's ok. I**'m / am making** a poster about 'Five Famous People from Wales' at the moment.
Mrs Sinclair	And **have you already found** any information you can use?

Answer key

Bex	Yes, I have! The oldest famous Welsh person I have found is King Arthur. Before he pulled the famous sword out of a stone and became the new king, there **had been** many battles with the country's enemies.
Mrs Sinclair	When did King Arthur live?
Bex	I don't know exactly when he **lived**. But I'm sure that he **had died** before my next famous Welsh person was born. His name is Thomas Myddelton.
Mrs Sinclair	Isn't this the one who lived in Chirk Castle?
Bex	That's right. Before Thomas Myddelton **bought** Chirk Castle in 1595, he **had worked** as a grocer in London. Until he **made** a lot of money from the East India Company, he had not been very rich. His family lived in the Castle for more than 300 years.
Mrs Sinclair	Does the family still live there today?
Bex	I don't know! Anyway, our next person is very famous, too!
Mrs. Sinclair	Who are you talking about?
Bex	**I'm / am talking** about George Everest. Sir George Everest.
Mrs. Sinclair	Everest? Like the world's highest mountain?
Bex:	Exactly. Sir George Everest **was** a famous Welsh person who lived in the 18th century. Before his family moved to London, he **had spent** his childhood in Wales. It is not even clear whether he was born in Wales, but his family had owned a house there before they **went** to London.
Mrs Sinclair:	That's interesting! I didn't know that!
Bex:	As you said before, Mum, the world's highest mountain – Mount Everest – was named after him, but Everest's name was a compromise because the Indian people **had already used** many different names for the mountain.
Mrs Sinclair:	So Mr Everest was really proud that they wanted to use his name for the mountain, wasn't he?
Bex:	No, not really! Sir George **didn't like** the idea at first as he **had had** nothing to do with the discovery of the mountain and he **thought** his name was difficult to pronounce and write in the Hindi language.
Mrs Sinclair:	Oh, I see. So, who is your next famous person?
Bex:	It's a boxer called Jimmy Wilde. It was Dad's idea. You know, he is a great fan of boxing and he **knows** everything about Welsh sports. Jimmy Wilde was born in Cardiff, which had always been the industrial centre of Wales. Dad told me that before Wilde **became** the world lightweight champion in 1923, **he had fought** in hundreds of fights. **Have you ever heard** of him?
Mrs Sinclair	No, I haven't, actually. I'm not really interested in boxing, but more into music and films.
Bex	Great! Then you **will like** my fifth famous Welsh person!
Mrs Sinclair	Is it an actress? Is it Catherine Zeta-Jones, for example?
Bex	No, it's a singer and songwriter! Our last famous Welsh person is Duffy. Did you know that she was very unhappy when her family moved to England because she **hadn't wanted** to leave Wales? Just like Everest! Until her family moved to England, Duffy **had never spoken** English, but Welsh! She said that it had been really hard to learn it until she made some English-speaking friends at her new school.
Mrs Sinclair	Oh, poor girl!
Bex	Yes, I agree. That's why I must go now and **meet** some of my own English-speaking friends.

2 Vocabulary (12 CP, pp. 46–52)

12 CP (1 CP pro richtige Lücke)

Mr Summers	So David, you haven't done your homework again! I'm really **concerned / annoyed**!
David	I'm sorry, Mr Summers. I couldn't do it yesterday because I was cleaning the floor in the kitchen and then it was wet and **slippery** and I fell down. I had an accident!
Mr Summers	I see. So you are not an **experienced** cleaner?
David	No, I'm not. And after I had fallen down I was feeling **dizzy**, too, and my face turned very **pale**.
Mr Summers	David, I am really **relieved** that you were able to come to school today!
David	Yes, I know, Mr Summers, you are really not **amused**. But I was absolutely **terrified** because I thought I had to go to hospital!
Mr Summers	But David, don't be so **frantic**! I'm actually **amazed** about your imagination!
David	Well, … I'm sorry, Mr Summers, don't be **annoyed** with me. I promise to be more **ambitious** with my homework next time!

3 Mediation (30 CP; pp. 52/53)

Individuelle Antworten in Form einer E-Mail mit folgenden Aspekten:

- Formalia einer E-Mail (Kopf, Anrede, Schlussformel)
- Beantwortung der fünf Fragen:
  – Kann man auch eine Besichtigungstour mit dem Schiff machen?
  – Welche Informationen über Regensburg stehen auf der Homepage – ist es eine interessante Stadt?
  – Was kostet die Schiffstour?
  – Kann man auf dem Schiff etwas essen?
  – Können die Sinclairs ihren Hund Coco mitbringen?

Schulaufgabe 7

1 Listening comprehension (pp. 54/55)

1 (8 CP; 1 CP pro richtige Antwort; 1 CP pro korrigierte falsche Antwort)

	right	wrong
1 The capital of Colorado is Denver.	☒	☐
2 Denver is called 'mile high city' because it's just one mile away from the Rocky Mountains.	☐	☒
Denver is one mile above sea level.		
3 Arizona is the largest city in the US West because 700,000 people live there.	☐	☒
The population of Denver is 700,000 people.		
4 Altogether, there are three swimming pools at the Recreation Centre.	☒	☐
5 Inside the gymnasium, you can play volleyball, basketball and climb up a climbing wall.	☐	☒
The climbing wall is outdoors.		

2 (3 CP; 1 CP pro richtige Antwort)

1 The climbing wall
☐ closes in April until November.
☐ is closed from April until November.
☐ is only open in April and November.
☒ is closed from November until April.

2 Gary is surprised that
☒ many teenagers prefer the salad bar over the Mexican restaurant.
☐ so many people eat at the Mexican restaurant.
☐ nobody notices that most of the food was frozen.
☐ Western people often eat tacos and tortillas.

3 Gary likes best about the Recreation Center
☐ that you can see the Denver skyscrapers from the terrace.
☐ that the entrance fees are quite low.
☒ that it's eco-friendly.
☐ that it is really modern.

3 (7 CP; 1 CP pro richtige Lücke)
solar, fossil fuels, emissions, footprint, reusable, cutlery, waste

4 (4 CP; max. 2 CP pro richtige Antwort)
Beispiellösung:
1 It means that if you want to protect the environment it is *very important* to use sustainable methods, like reducing plastic or using solar energy.
2 *individuelle Lösungen*

2 Use of English (On / Fast Track, pp. 55–58)

(30 CP; 1 CP pro richtige Lücke)

Chris Mrs Golding said our part of the 'Route 66 Project' is the state of Arizona, right?
Kelly That's right. Arizona and New Mexico, too.
Chris If our topic **had been** the state of California, we **could have written** about Hollywood!
Kelly Yeah, but Arizona is an interesting state, too. Did you know that some parts of Arizona are still quite **unspoilt**? If we **find** enough information, we **can write** about the Grand Canyon.
Chris Cool! Let's do some internet research. We'**ll / will be** more effective if you **sit down** right next to me.
Kelly OK. Where can we start? Let's type 'Grand Canyon' into the search engine. Uuuh, so many results! If we **want** to finish today, we **must think** of a different search strategy.
Chris Good. Last week, Mrs Golding **said** that there is a glass platform over the Grand Canyon … I can't remember its name!
Kelly If you **had paid** more attention, we **wouldn't have wasted** so much time already!
Chris I'm sorry … But wait – I think it was called 'The Grand Canyon Skywalk'.
Kelly Great. Let's see. Here. The text says that the Grand Canyon Skywalk is located on the Western **rim** of the Grand Canyon, on the Hualapai Indian Reservation, and it **opened** in 2007. It is 4,000 feet above the ground. Tourists need a **permit** if they **take** pictures.
Chris The Hualapai tribe actually saw some **advantages** in the Skywalk, didn't they?
Kelly Yes, they did. Many of the Native Americans **had been** unemployed for ages before the opening of the Skywalk. Look at what one of them is saying today: 'If the Skywalk **hadn't brought** so many tourists to the area, unemployment **would have continued**.'
Chris But some **environmentalists** said no one knew what **impact** the Skywalk would have on nature. It's important that you behave respectfully towards nature.
Kelly That's right. Let's see what else we can use.
Chris The website also says that tourists **will enjoy** amazing views of the Grand Canyon if they **book** a helicopter ride.
Kelly Well, I'**d / would like** to watch the **sunset** over the Grand Canyon. I'm sure that's really romantic! What **would you do** if you ever **went** to the Grand Canyon?
Chris I don't know … If I **won** the lottery, I **would try** all the activities!

3 Mediation (30 CP; pp. 59/60)

Individuelle Antworten

Schulaufgabe 8

1 Reading comprehension (pp. 61–65)

1 (8 CP; 1 CP pro richtige Antwort; 1 CP pro korrigierte falsche Antwort)

	right	wrong
1 In the Super Bowl competition, the winner of the AFC and the winner of the NFL play against each other.	☐	☒

The winner of the AFC and the winner of the NFC play against each other.

	right	wrong
2 The people riding rodeos are called 'broncos'.	☐	☒

The horses are called broncos.

	right	wrong
3 Lilac often watches the Broncos' games at the stadium in Denver.	☒	☐
4 The Denver Broncos have won the Super Bowl three times.	☒	☐
5 You can use the term 'Bowl' only for NFL games.	☐	☒

'Bowl' can be used for any major American football game.

2 (4 CP; 1 CP pro richtige Antwort)

1 The Super Bowl trophy
☐ has always been silver.
☐ has been golden since the year 2016.
☐ is silver and golden at the same time.
☒ is normally silver, but not in the year 2016.

2 The 51st Super Bowl competition
☐ took place in 2018.
☒ had the number 'LI'.
☐ had a clear winner: the Denver Broncos
☐ didn't get a Roman number.

3 In January 2016,
☐ the New England Patriots won against the Denver Broncos.
☐ the Carolina Panthers won the Super Bowl.
☒ the Denver Broncos won against the New England Patriots.
☐ the Denver Broncos won the Super Bowl.

4 In Mile High Stadium,
☐ more than 90,500 people can watch the games.
☒ concerts and other sports events take place.
☐ there are more soccer games than American football games.
☐ the most expensive seat is one mile above the ground.

3 (4 CP; max. 2 CP pro vervollständigte Antwort)

1 … the term 'bowl' originated in Pasadena, CA, the Denver Broncos of Colorado are the most successful team at the moment, and the 50th anniversary Super Bowl took place in Santa Clara, CA, which the Denver Broncos won.

2 … she was the first female artist to have a concert there, and the revenue was also the highest ever in the history of the stadium.

4 (4 CP; max. 2 CP pro vervollständigte Antwort)

1 Lilac uses 'unfortunately' to express that she is a little frustrated that the Super Bowl 50 game didn't take place at Mile High stadium in Denver. If the game had been in Denver, she might have watched it live.

2 Lilac chose a fancy name for her blog, her entries are not too long (100–200 words), she posts regularly every week, but sometimes her language is quite complicated and she also posts much personal information. It would be safer if she used an avatar instead.

5 (4 CP; 2 CP pro Frage)

Mögliche Antworten:
- What is the best part of the Super Bowl festivities?
- Is there a women's American football league?
- Did you visit any of the concerts at Mile High?

2 Use of English (On / Fast Track, pp. 66–70)

1 (24 CP; 1 CP pro richtige Lücke)

Caleb Lilac, you said in the interview that you like the fourth of July holiday best. Why?

Lilac It's mainly because I love the fireworks, and also because my aunt and uncle visit us every year on the fourth of July. If they **didn't come** on the fourth of July, I **wouldn't see** them at all!
But of course I also like the fourth of July because of its history. The United States of America **wouldn't even exist** if the thirteen original colonies in New England **hadn't declared** independence on the fourth of July in the year 1776.

Caleb Yes, that's true. And we **would still belong to** Great Britain if the Founding Fathers **hadn't signed** the Declaration of Independence!

Lilac Yeah, that's a funny thought, isn't it?

Caleb When I **watch** the fireworks on the next fourth of July, I**'ll / will surely think** of it!

Lilac Caleb, what's your favorite holiday? If **I remember** correctly, it **was** Thanksgiving, wasn't it?

Caleb Yes, that's right. I guess we'd all be very unhappy if we **couldn't celebrate** Thanksgiving. We love the food! Especially the roast turkey, of course.

Lilac I'm sure the turkey **would be** happier if you **ate** less meat …

Caleb Oh, Lilac! Are you a vegetarian now? Let me tell you something about the first Thanksgiving, you know, it **happened** in 1621. The Pilgrims – that's the name of the first settlers – and the Native Americans **were sitting** together, at one table. They **thanked** God that they were still alive! If the Native Americans **hadn't shown** the Pilgrims how to grow corn and catch fish, they **wouldn't have survived** the first year in America.

Lilac So, **do you usually help** with the food on Thanksgiving?

Caleb	Well, a little bit. If I **have** time, I **chop** the vegetables. Until I **learn** how to cook a turkey properly, my Mum **will do / will have to do** it.
Lilac	But just imagine: What would happen if you **became** a vegetarian?
Caleb	No way!

2 (10 CP; 1 CP pro richtige Antwort)

persuaded us to do, compared, recommended, to sequence our ideas, delivered, offend, reviewed, supervised, affected, conduct

3 Writing (p. 70)

Max. 30 CP

Individuelle Lösungen in Form einer E-Mail mit folgenden Aspekten:

- Formalia einer E-Mail (Kopf, Anrede, Schlussformel)
- Informationen zu allen vier Aspekten (dein Job, die indigene Bevölkerung, Ökotourismus; deine Schule; deine Pläne für den Rest des Jahres; was daran deinen Freunden gefallen bzw. nicht gefallen würde)

Acknowledgements

Picture credits

|alamy images, Abingdon/Oxfordshire: Andronov, Leonid 53; B Christopher 24; Buzz Pictures 41, 42; Clarence Holmes Photography 66, 68; Cotterill, Alick 44; Cultura Creative (RF) 32, 33; Herrett, Roberto 45; Mathews, Terry 44; MicaUK 44; Munoz, Juan Carlos 55, 57; Segre, Alex 22; Sinclair, Paulette 22; Woman filling cup at water cooler 16; Zoonar GmbH 16. |Dölling, Andrea, Berlin: 31. |Donnelly, Karen, Brighton: 9, 10, 12, 17, 18. |Eyferth, Konrad, Berlin: 31. |fotolia.com, New York: Do Ra 39; HaveZein 39; monticelllo 16. |Getty Images, München: Yellow Dog Productions 61. |iStockphoto.com, Calgary: AngelMcNallphotography 55, 57; clu 27, 28; ioanmasay 31. |Marckwort, Ulf, Kassel: 30, 31. |Naumann, Andrea, Aachen: 32, 33. |Shutterstock.com, New York: Adamson, David 46, 49; Sohm, Joseph 62; Vectorin 61. |stock.adobe.com, Dublin: Africa Studio 16; Alexander 22; alho007 22; goldencow_images 16; makam1969 38; masanyanka 30; michelaubryphoto 16; Prostock-studio 21; sahua d 16; Yantra 16.

Wir arbeiten sehr sorgfältig daran, für alle verwendeten Abbildungen die Rechteinhaberinnen und Rechteinhaber zu ermitteln. Sollte uns dies im Einzelfall nicht vollständig gelungen sein, werden berechtigte Ansprüche selbstverständlich im Rahmen der üblichen Vereinbarungen abgegolten.

Audios

Dialogues recorded at Air-Edel Studios, London.
Produced by Anne Rosenfeld for RBA Productions.
Recording engineer: Mark Smith